I0201008

AUSTIN'S CABIN

Clinging to Hope

Paulette Reed

Austin's Cabin
Copyright © 2026 Paulette Reed

All Rights Reserved. No part of this publication may be reproduced, stored in a retrieval system or transmitted in any form or by any means – electronic, mechanical, photocopy, recording or any other – except for brief quotations in printed reviews, without the prior permission of the author.

Unless otherwise noted, scripture quotations are from The Passion Translation®. Copyright © 2017, 2018, 2020 by Passion & Fire Ministries, Inc. Used by permission. All rights reserved. ThePassionTranslation.com.

Scripture quotations marked NIV are taken from Holy Bible, New International Version®, NIV® Copyright ©1973, 1978, 1984, 2011 by Biblica, Inc.® Used by permission. All rights reserved worldwide.

New American Standard Bible®. Copyright © The Lockman Foundation 1960, 1962, 1963, 1968, 1971, 1972, 1973, 1975, 1977, 1995.

Scripture quotations marked NKJV are taken from the New King James Version®. Copyright © 1982 by Thomas Nelson. Used by permission.

Scripture quotations marked NLT are taken from The Holy Bible, New Living Translation, copyright © 1996, 2004, 2015 by Tyndale House Foundation. Used by permission of Tyndale House Publishers, Inc.

I am deeply grateful to my editor, Carol Martinez, for her encouragement, professional guidance, and careful editorial judgment, which greatly contributed to the completion of this work.
Carol Anne Martinez
Free Lance Editing/Publishing/Design
Carol.MartinezCarter@gmail.com

Cover artwork and sketches by:

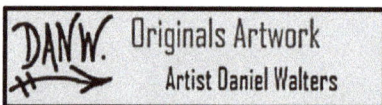

DANW. Originals Artwork
Artist Daniel Walters

Facebook: DanW Originals Artwork

Published by Paulette Reed Ministry
PauletteReed.com
ISBN: 979-8-218-89122-0

Now may God, the inspiration and fountain of hope,
fill you to overflowing with uncontainable joy
and perfect peace as you trust in him.
And may the power of the Holy Spirit continually
surround your life with his super-abundance until
you radiate with hope! —Romans 15:13

Dedication

*To my family, who remind me that love
is the greatest legacy.*

TABLE OF CONTENTS

INTRODUCTION

What Is Grief, Really?

Merriam-Webster defines grief as:

(a) deep and poignant distress caused by or as if by bereavement, and
(b) a cause of such suffering.

To me, that definition of grief seems far too inadequate. Grief expands beyond what any language can express. It doesn't simply make us sad; it grips us with heartache that words cannot explain.

Shock and Surreal Moments

As I grieved, I recall our Campus Pastor, Heather, a compassionate friend and mother of two beautiful little boys, gently saying, "I just can't imagine."

I turned to her and whispered, "I can't either."

The whole calamity felt surreal, a waking nightmare with no way out. I kept hoping to wake up and see my son. I longed to talk with him, hug him, tell him I loved him.

I struggled to breathe. Inhale. Exhale.

And yet, somehow, missions were accomplished. Arrangements and details completed.

Helping hands stepped forward and carried the burden with me, for which I will be forever grateful.

And then … silence.

The Empty Chair

Wait. What about the empty chair?

What about the pain that refuses to leave?

What about the huge hole in my heart, invisible to the world but consuming to me?

Some days dragged on endlessly. Others passed quickly but in a heavy fog.

I was lost, unsure what to do with a heart that had been crushed.

I hated, hated the permanence of death.

Still, I kept moving, step by step, choosing to trust that God's peace waited ahead.

Grief Breaks the Rules

I view myself as a stable person.

Over the years, I had learned how to manage my emotions instead of letting them rule me.

But grief threw the rule book out the window.

Often, I couldn't even finish a sentence without crying.

It seemed ridiculous, irritating, to say the least.

Would this wild ride last forever? Or would it stop?

The tears came anytime, anyplace—Walmart, church, a basketball game, the grocery store.

Any tiny object that reminded me of him, any spoken or read word could trigger a tsunami of tears.

Often, I thought I was okay until someone asked, "Are you okay?" And then I fell apart.

I began to wonder if all the king's horses and all the king's men could put me back together again. What's the plan here, God? Help!

Rollercoaster of Emotions

I had never encountered such a wild rollercoaster of emotions.

As time passed, some days I thought, "Hey, maybe I will survive this."

Then, the very next morning, I'd wake up thinking,

"What do I need to do today just to stay out of a psychiatric unit?"

Yes, dramatic. But also, honest.

That irrational rollercoaster dragged me along, day after day.

Fortunately, down deep I knew that tears help wash away the pain, and joy comes in the morning (Psalm 35).

Above all, I knew from Scripture that God promises to mend the brokenhearted, and I clung to that promise.

God cannot lie.

Limited Human Understanding

Even if people listened to my pain, most of them struggled to understand the depths of grief.

Support groups helped since we were all members of a club we never chose to join.

We bonded, cried, and laughed together.

Each time we shared, we healed.

I don't think our culture fosters healing from grief very well. Corporate America often allows three to five days of paid bereavement leave when a close loved one dies. That could establish a harmful standard on a national level.

Seriously, *three to five days* for a shattered heart to heal?

Come on. Even broken bones take six weeks to heal.

Let's do better.

Writing Through the Pain

I also realized that writing helped me heal.

God was my lifeline, and journaling helped me process my feelings.

I found a way to cry onto the page when I couldn't sort through the chaos in my mind.

Writing letters to my son helped the pain and feelings escape from my mind, body, and soul.

I called some of my journaling *Letters to Heaven*.

This book contains some of those letters.

From there, I'll share how His grace carried me when I couldn't carry myself.

I'll talk about the deafening silence that sometimes surrounded me and how the world responded to my loss...or chose not to.

I'll try to reach for your hand and walk with *you* through the valley of the shadow of death (Psalm 23).

And I'll do my best to offer you a safe place, as a friend who gets it.

Dear God,

Love,
Paulette

Chapter One

SHOCK

Every Parent's Worst Nightmare

We all have moments in life that shatter our hearts.

We must learn to navigate journeys we never wanted to take.

I laid my phone back on the nightstand when I noticed the caller ID: **Unpublished.**

It was 10:24 p.m.

I thought, "This must be a prank call. A scammer."

I yawned, unaware that this phone call would change my life forever.

I was tired. I had spent the day preparing for a five-hour drive to see my firstborn son.

The oil in my car was changed.

I filled the gas tank.

I shopped, cleaned, laundered, and packed.

Everything was ready for the trip.

The phone rang again.

Then again.

By the third call, annoyance turned to dread.

This time, the screen showed an Iowa number.

My heart pounded as I answered.

It was the sheriff's office.

Words no one ever wants to hear.

Hearing the Unthinkable

A young deputy, likely delivering one of his first horrific notifications, spoke with a trembling voice. He hadn't yet built the emotional callousness the job demands. Unfortunately, there was no buffer. No preamble. Just devastating news.

"Ms. Reed?"

"Yes."

"This is Officer Somebody from the County Sheriff's Office...

"It seems your son, Austin, didn't show up for work. This evening, we received a call from a friend of his asking us to do a welfare check. When we went into his cabin, we found him inside ... deceased."

Wait. What?!

He kept speaking, but I only remember fragments.

"No. No. No." That's all I could say.

Shock surged. My thoughts unraveled.

One word echoed: *deceased.*

He asked me to grab a pen.

Somehow, I did.

I scribbled the name and number of the coroner—

a coroner, of all things.

Please, God, let this be a nightmare I can wake up from.

Before hanging up, he apologized for giving me the news by phone.

Maybe a knock at the door would have been worse. I'll never know.

The Aftermath

My hands shook as I called my other two sons. There's just no good way to tell somebody their loved one has died.

They arrived quickly. They hugged me so tightly I could hardly breathe. I felt my knees buckle from trauma, but their strong arms held me upright.

We talked.

We cried.

The coroner said the cardiac arrest and passing were instant. Austin was exhausted from the battle of life, and his body simply gave out.

I paced in circles whispering, *"I just don't know what to do."*

After my two sons left to rest, I pulled out boxes and boxes and photos. I sat on the floor for hours, surrounded by memories.

There it all was. Austin's baby book, swing sets and sand boxes, his kindergarten picture in the red cowboy shirt he insisted on wearing, Christmases with his brothers, lots of kittens, bicycles, go-carts, and minibikes. There were football pictures, wrestling trophies, fishing trips, university pics, firefighter days, award certificates, skilled tradesman completions and of course, tons of photos of him with his precious children, Gabriel and Trinity. It was as if time stood still. The air got strangely quiet, and grief settled in beside me as I turned each page. Every picture hurt in a tender way only love can, as though each snapshot whispered that my life as I knew it had moved on, and I could never step back into it again. The line of demarcation was permanent.

Light eventually crept through the window. *Oh. The sun's coming up.* I didn't feel tired at all, but of course I went ahead and made coffee. Coffee helps most everything.

Unfortunately however, there wasn't a single piece of chocolate in the house. That had to change quickly.

Beginning the Journey

The day my son passed away had passed away. Mercy and Love held me as I grabbed a notebook and made a travel list.

The trip to see my son had changed in the worst possible way.

I also made a list of people I needed to call.

No guidebook on earth teaches you how to say, *"My son has died. He's gone."*

How do you speak those words?

Please, Lord. I need grace, empowerment from heaven, to make it through this.

Autopilot engaged. All I could do was place one foot in front of another ... step-by-step. I asked God to take over. And of course He stepped in, as He faithfully had done for decades.

He showered me with grace from Above.

A Word of Hope

Losing a child, even an adult child, shatters a person in ways few can grasp. No parent should ever have to bury their child. Ever.

I know the terrain of grief better than I care to admit. Within six years, I had lost my mother and father, and now most painfully, my son.

In that same timespan, promises were broken—huge promises. I lost relationships with people I love, and I left behind nearly all possessions. I found myself surrounded by uncertainty and a sea of strangers, but also by the love of family, and above all, the steadfast love of God. I didn't do everything right while walking through the valley of darkness. Neither will you. Still, God keeps us. He's always gracious.

When the storms quiet, He promises beauty for ashes.

I, for one, am holding out for that season.

How about you?

A Hand to Hold

I know you have your own valleys to walk through.

As you do, please hear this:

I'm so deeply sorry. Truly I am.

I send you my deepest sympathy and compassion. I lift you in prayer.

I believe with all my heart you will survive this.

Every crisis has a beginning and an end.

Cling to that. Cling to Hope.

It will not always be this hard, so don't let the hard days win.

And when the time is right, turn off the autopilot … and live again.

After all, I'm still here.

And hey, I'm writing this book for you.

One breath.

One step.

One moment at a time.

Eventually, those steps lead you a great distance.

I know it's important to keep moving forward, but the truth is, I really miss my son.

Sometimes the ache of his absence catches me off guard, and the only way I know to work through that right now is by writing.

So I thought I'd share a bit of that journaling.

Maybe, just maybe, it'll help someone else too.

KEY TAKEWAY

When you don't know what to do, slow your breathing. Inhale. Exhale. And just do the next right thing.

MY JOURNAL

MY JOURNAL

Chapter Two

"I MISS YOU"

Letters to Heaven

Journaling can help us process raw feelings we don't know what to do with.

Pouring out pain helps keep us lucid. Pouring out love helps keep it alive.

Good morning, Austin,

I miss you. I mean I really, really miss you. It feels like someone opened my chest, took my heart out, and shattered it into pieces. The words broken heart carry a whole new meaning for me; shock and deep grief crush everything inside. A sharp pain pierces this mother's heart—a level of sorrow I've never known. All I can say is, thank God He stays close to the brokenhearted (Psalm 34:18). I can't imagine surviving without Him. He's real. He helps.

During my walk last night, anger seemed to be my companion, a stage of grief I wish I could bypass. I did not like seeing people ride bikes with their kids or watching a family play with their dog. Instead, I hurt. I felt robbed of time on earth with you. This whole situation strikes me as too stinkin' permanent! It's so not fair. I'm learning that grief is much more than just missing someone; it's a deep ache for life to be different and for the impossible to come true.

As I walked, I shouted into the air, "I want to see Austin! I want to talk to Austin!" I needed to scream, yell, hit something, or someone. I longed to see my firstborn son. Does anybody hear me? Does anybody care?

Tears flowed as I finished my walk. When I got home, I grabbed your beautiful, beat-up college wrestling sweatshirt we found hanging on a nail in your garage. It may be well over twenty years old, but I cherish it like a brand-new gift from heaven. I, too, must wrestle. I must wrestle through this. Don't give up. Keep going. Stay strong and take courage, I tell myself. This pain won't last forever. I clutch your shirt, hug it tightly, and try to rest.

I've listened to TED Talks about grief. Some resonate; some are weird. I try to take slow, intentional steps and pray for discernment. I know I'm vulnerable right now, and strange people with magic-potion promises show up in these moments. It's a delicate time, a time to be incredibly careful with my heart.

Focus is difficult to come by right now, but I reach for every sliver of solace I can grab. How did this happen? How do I continue without all of My Three Sons? Just typing those words stings. I always loved saying "My Three Sons," my greatest earthly accomplishment, my flesh and blood. With each miraculous birth, I discovered the meaning of love. I feel so proud of all of you.

Your brothers miss you, Austin. We all do—your children, family, and friends. I wish you had known how much people loved *you. Maybe you did. At your celebration of life, your friend Chris said he believed you carried all that love tucked away somewhere. The outpouring of sympathy and compassion was touching. People filled the rooms, and cards and memorial gifts for your children continue to show up. We are so grateful.*

I thank God for you. I will find ways to build a lasting legacy of your life until we reunite in heaven, face to face with Jesus. Please tell Him hi for me.

You'll be happy to know we're looking after Gabriel and Trinity. I know how much you adored them, and they adored you. Thank you for making sure they remain cared for. Even in the midst of struggle, you did so many things right. Love shines through your children. Oh, and did I mention? They are perfect grandchildren. Smile.

Oh wow! I just realized something. In a way, I did get to talk to you. I did!

Love you,
Ma

Note: When I share my letters to heaven here, it could seem like I'm talking directly to my son, so just a gentle word of caution to protect you, please. Journaling provides a place for our feelings to land, but the Bible teaches us that we should never talk to the deceased. The reason being, there are familiar spirits (demons) who have a limited ability to imitate things about the deceased and even speak through people—mediums for example. Evil spirits prey on hurting, vulnerable people and pretend to comfort. but in the long run they are always out to destroy. There is only one Holy Spirit, the third person of the Trinity. He is an active helper, intercessor, translator, and even initiator of prayer, mediating between humans and the presence of God.

The Healing Process

I feel grateful for the nudge to journal, something I haven't done in a while. We all need ways to push through emotional pain, and writing helps. Pushing through might feel impossible right now, and that's okay. Don't force it. Just keep life simple and treat yourself with kindness. Seasons of grief call for gentle care.

Sometimes our world feels like it stops. But trust me, the earth still rotates, the sun still rises in glory, and new lives continue to enter the world every day.

The time will come when you feel ready to move forward, knowing deep down that life holds more than grief and trauma. Love, laughter, and success *will wait for you* until you release the pause button.

People need you, family, friends, colleagues, all wait for your full presence. However, this process takes time, so be careful not to let guilt slip in. Go at your pace and don't let people take that from you. We all grieve differently. Later we'll talk about the stages of grief. They can help us see whether we're grieving in a healthy way or need to make changes.

Emotional Honesty

Journaling should help us understand ourselves, not shift blame. What's really going on inside? Why are we quite so angry? Why do we feel so mistreated or discombobulated?

You've probably heard it said that certain people or events "push our buttons." Well, let's heal until there are no more buttons to push.

We're adults now. We can learn life skills that carry us through the issues of life.

Sometimes grief reveals our weaknesses. Character flaws may surface when we're hurting and have no strength to mask them. We're just too tired to hide them, and that can be a good thing. Journaling can bring healthy conviction about what we're dealing with. No condemnation allowed. "Oh dear, there's that old anger again. Oh, there I go overcontrolling a situation again." Understandable, we are trying to fix a painful situation, but there is a right way and a wrong way. Or maybe there's no way; some things just can't be fixed. Perhaps it's time to honestly recognize old patterns popping up and then break the patterns so we're free. Free to heal, free to live and love.

Finding Purpose

Even our strengths can become weaknesses when overextended. Confidence, overhelping, communication, they can all go sideways in a crisis. Journaling helps us see what's happening so we can start making better choices.

Tragedy will shake us, but we don't have to allow it to overtake us. Over time we will learn to find purpose in the pain. And someday, we'll help others, *because how could we not, knowing what we know?* Once we know deep grief, we recognize suffering more acutely.

Destiny Awaits

Dreaming about your God-given destiny as the storm settles can help you keep going. Maybe it's time to recalculate. Most professionals say to wait a year after crises before making big decisions, and that's wise. But they don't say we can't dream. Listen, you'll know you're healing when you start dreaming again.

What stirs your heart? What's your passion? Those things didn't change in the storm. They're still in you, waiting to be attended to. They will be there when you're strong again and ready to step out in faith.

Healing matters. Scripture says we prosper and enjoy good health *as our soul prospers* (3 John 1:2). That truth alone should spark incredible motivation to heal. Let's make sure our mind, emotions, and will thrive so we can too.

Healthy Expression

If journaling isn't for you, maybe try voice recordings, art, music, sticky notes or whatever helps you process. Let your feelings land somewhere healthy.

When the sheriff's office called me, trauma and grief struck instantaneously. Of course, not all grief arrives that way. Sometimes it comes gently, like when someone who is a hundred years old passes away. The grief is there, but perhaps little or no trauma because the passing was expected. But when loss blindsides us, trauma and grief arrive together.

Imagine grief as getting hit by a semi-truck because that's what it feels like. Would you expect to just slap on a band-aid and walk it off? Of course not. Deep wounds require deep healing. We don't want pain covered up; we want it healed! That process takes work and cooperation on our part. You can do it. I believe in you.

At first, I didn't know how I'd survive the pain of grief. But it does get better. **I promise**. Will we always miss our loved ones? Absolutely. Of course. However, we can learn to use our suffering to inspire change—for ourselves and for others. Grief can actually make us a different person, a better person … if we let it. Ironic, I know. It's the crushing of the grape that causes sweetness to flow.

Emotional Awareness

As an experienced administrator, I've learned that keeping things simple helps us get from Point A to Point Z well—simply. As you heal, just keep doing the next right thing. Keep heading toward the finish line at the end of that dark valley, even if there are days you can only crawl.

Grief clouds our view, but identifying emotions helps clear the fog. At the core, there are only four emotions: mad, sad, glad, and scared. Pinpointing what we're feeling and the intensity of these emotions makes them manageable. Are you a little angry, agitated, or furious? Uneasy or paralyzed, needing assistance to move?

Once we can answer those questions, we begin making wiser choices. No unhealthy coping mechanisms allowed. Say it with me: "I don't do that anymore." It's actually a relief to identify emotions, and journaling can be a powerful tool for this. Suddenly, our feelings don't seem out of control.

For me, during the initial stages of grief, sleep was my only respite, and I welcomed it. For you, maybe it's time for some fun. When was the last time you laughed with a friend or watched a great comedy? Find out what gives you *healthy* rest from the pain and cherish it.

What to Do

When we come to understand what we're feeling and why, what's next? We can try to determine what to do with our emotions, but don't stress, it takes time.

Perhaps it's time to ...

- Forgive someone or yourself.

- Recognize if or when we're ruminating and do what we must to stop.

- If our needs aren't being met, ask ourselves how we can begin to change that?

- Seek professional help.

- Let go and let God. Some things cannot be fixed by humanness.

All this emotional processing helps you gauge the level of support you might need. Sometimes journaling is enough. Sometimes it's not. And that's okay. Pain just doesn't disappear. So let's face it, work through it, and release it.

Dear Austin,

Today I tried to recall all the promises of God I decreed over you for decades. Scripture says the Word of God holds power and must accomplish what it was sent out (spoken) to do.

Even though I can no longer see you, I know those decrees were answered because the word of God never returns void. It's interesting. Now you're at perfect peace in heaven. I am so encouraged when others send me scriptures for support, infusing me with God's promises as I grieve—oh, how I need them! Sure, I can find them in the Bible myself, but there is something special about someone sending these words ... like God speaking through them. Every act of kindness is a step toward healing a broken heart.

I'm so glad I texted you scriptures just before you passed. Every time you responded, I felt joy. I know I got on your nerves sometimes, okay, more than sometimes, but you received Truth, and that blesses me. Shortly before you died, you replied after I texted you a scripture saying, "That's a good one!" And it was.

It sure was an honor to be your mom.

Love you,
Ma

The Answers Within

We all search for answers, but the truth is, they're often right inside us. When we invite the Lord into our hearts, Holy Spirit moves in and is *always* our Helper, our Comforter. His Spirit lives in us so as we journal or process externally with someone and wisdom and revelation rise to the surface.

Sometimes, when I listen to someone pour out their heart, longing for answers, I can tell by the expression on their face that they just received the answer to their own question. That's powerful.

The Bond

I also joined a grief support group, where I found others who, like me, were learning to live with loss. We were all finding our way through pain, together. I came to appreciate those gatherings where I was free to talk. Grief, after all, is love with nowhere to go. When we lose someone, we carry that love inside us, still longing to share it. Please, let me talk about my son.

Science now confirms what a mother's heart always knew: we share an eternal bond with our children. Through something called *microchimerism*,[1] we carry their cells inside us, sometimes for life.

I always believed God would fully free my son from everything that didn't come from Him. And He did. Not my way, but His. Thy will be done.

I remember sitting on my couch shortly after Austin passed away, thinking aloud, "Lord, You could have healed him here on earth."

Immediately God whispered to my heart:

"Paulette, Austin wanted to come home."

Wow. How do you argue with that?

It's wonderful to know the Lord is always with us, and it seems He proves that most when we need Him most. When the heartache feels overwhelming, His presence slips in with comfort, filling us with hope to cling to.

KEY TAKEAWAY

"Lord, you have always been our eternal home ... "
(Psalm 90:1).

MY JOURNAL

MY JOURNAL

Chapter Three

THE FINGERPRINTS OF GOD

Man's Best Friend

What we fix our eyes on begins to shape our world.

Let's fix our eyes on Jesus.

Dear Austin,

Sleep escapes me tonight, so I thought I would write for a while.

When the sheriff's office called a few weeks ago, my circadian rhythm was disrupted. I didn't sleep at all for about three days. I didn't feel exhausted; sleep just did not come. Sometimes it still doesn't. Not a humongous problem, but it throws me off socially. If I get up at 3 a.m., and someone wants to go to lunch at noon, I'm ready for a nap, not lunch. This too shall pass.

You know I'm very visual, so pictures really bring me comfort. I spend a lot of time looking at photos of our family and smiling or crying, it depends on the moment. I also spend a lot of time praying. I want answers. I'll sleep better when God's supernatural peace takes over. I know it will. God's kind that way.

I don't know if you can see down here. There are some mysteries of the Kingdom of Heaven we're not supposed to know.

God's ways are higher than our ways. But if you could, you would be thrilled to know your beautiful German Shepherd is well taken care of.

What a miraculous journey it was to get Kanyon to an amazing home. It started with your brothers cleaning out your cabin. A couple of your friends helped, and one of them was interested in taking Kanyon home. She was anxious after you were gone, and we knew she needed someone gentle and trustworthy. We were grateful for the offer, but how could we be one hundred percent sure if that was the perfect match?

When everyone finished cleaning, the guys quickly put the dog in their truck and took off. Well, Kanyon had other plans, and it seems so did the Lord.

The next morning, your brother was driving with your cell phone and some keepsakes lying on the truck seat. Your cell phone kept ringing and ringing. He didn't know the passcode, but he saw the same number calling repeatedly. When he parked, he returned the call.

Get this: Kanyon had busted through a fence the night before and ran off. As she was wandering around town a gentleman who has trained German Shepherds for thirty years spotted her! He was calling to let us know that he had sat on the ground for about forty minutes, gently coaxing your little run away to come near. When she did, he fed her, loved her, and took her to the vet to have her chip read. Up came your name and phone number.

In a town of 22,000 people, a trainer of three decades finds your sweet dog. Wow. Godly coincidence has a name, it's Holy

Spirit. The Helper, or Paraclete in the Greek, comes alongside to provide comfort, support, and guidance.

The trainer really wanted to find a home for Kanyon; that's what he does. Kanyon was placed with a couple who had lost their own German Shepherd of ten years and, sadly, they had also lost a son, like I did. They're active at a local shelter and have a veterinarian in the family. They said they're smitten with Kanyon. I think every pet should live in a home where people are smitten with them.

It's so comforting to know God is in the details. It's as if He's using a megaphone to speak into our pain: "I'm right here! I've got this. What's important to you is important to Me."

Now that is love.

I hope we all learn from this that life is fragile. We must embrace each day, weaving together the good, the bad, and the ugly— all under God's excellent care.

Please know: your pup is safe. And don't forget, God spelled backwards is d-o-g, man's best friend.

Love you,
Ma

White Buffalo

There was a season at the cabin when life looked promising. Realizing that seeking help is a sign of strength, my son sought help, and he changed. We all saw it. His eyes shone brighter. He carried a peace we hadn't seen in a long time. I was so thrilled to watch him begin to thrive. He made it through a painful divorce, made a nice home for himself and his children in a cabin he liked, and was a skilled tradesman. Things were looking good.

For years, he felt like the odd one out of the family. But he finally realized that was a lie, something we often told him. It was clear he had experienced a spiritual awakening. One tangible expression of this was how he changed his environment from dark to light. His new décor was white. His new truck was white. His yard ornaments were white, and he placed white buffalo decorations around his home.

Later, we learned the white buffalo holds deep symbolism in Native American tradition. It's a symbol of sacredness, hope, peace, and rebirth. It represents inner strength, courage, and grace. Because their birth is so rare, they are seen as miraculous signs, bridging heaven and earth.

A while after our loss, one of my other sons took a trip to Wyoming. The flight was over seven hundred miles. When he checked in and opened the door to his hotel room, sitting in the middle of a huge bed was a stuffed, eight-inch-tall white buffalo. And now it's on my bookshelf.

Oh, how God loves you! He's got this.

Dear Austin,

You've been gone six months now. It still seems unreal. My heart longs for a phone call, a text, or, better yet, a knock on the door. I love you. I miss you every day.

You had a good heart, and God looks at the heart (1 Samuel 16:7). I cling to the dream the Lord gave me of you in heaven. I saw you. I heard your voice. You looked healthy and radiant. I rejoice knowing that in heaven there is no pain, no sorrow, no tears (Revelation 21:4).

And I rejoice knowing everyone who invites Jesus into their heart will be in heaven for eternity. That's a long, long time. For now, I grieve. But I'm surrounded by loving family and friends, as we navigate this journey together.

I salute you for never giving up. You wrestled with life until the end. You won the ultimate victory. When we take our last breath on earth, we take our next in heaven.

Someday I will see you again!

Love you,
Ma

Note: I wrote the letter above on Saturday. Today is Monday. I heard a knock at my door a few minutes ago. I opened it and saw a new maintenance worker from our apartment complex. He seemed like a sweet young man.

He said, "Hello."

I said, "Hello, what's your name?"

He said, "Austin."

I could have fainted, in a good way.

God is omnipresent. He's kind, loving, caring, and comforting.

He knows the details of our lives.

Austin knocked on my door today.

Reframing the Pain

As I emerge from the fog of grief, I realize there will always be a before and after. But I can choose how to live with it. Grief and joy *can* coexist, woven together into my personal tapestry.

Grief is phase one. Reframing must be phase two. It's like renovating a home: demolition comes first, then rebuilding.

Our loved ones would not want us stuck in sorrow. We will learn to let the glow of love shine through the cracks of our hearts. And let's remember that what we dwell on, we enlarge. So, let's dwell on the joy of the time we had together.

More Fingerprints

For my son's special day, I bought a cupcake and sang "Happy Birthday." I hope he heard me.

Then I opened my treasure box and gently held each item: his driver's license, pocketknife, certificates, flashlight, socks, coins, and pictures. I looked at each item, remembering.

The hard truth is that the crisis has already happened. It's over. That won't change. So, I must. My son is gone. He's not coming back. Every part of me aches for that not to be true, but it is.

Second Samuel 12:23 frequently fills me with hope. David says of his deceased son, "Can I bring him back again? **I am going to him**, but he will not return to me."

When my mother passed, I gave my dad a beautiful blanket she had crocheted. He hugged it and asked the staff at the nursing home to never wash it. I understand that now. In fact, I read a story of a woman who put her dad's shirt in the freezer when he passed away. She could still smell his scent twenty years later. Amazing. We are created to love and be loved.

Birthdays and other special days are tough after we lose loved ones. I headed to bed early after my little celebration. As I closed my window blinds, I saw a pickup truck parked directly next to my car. It had an extended cab, same make, model, and color as Austin's. Iowa plates and from the same dealership, 335 miles away.

There it was—white and polished. I squinted to see if a white buffalo decal was on the back window. *Smile.*

God's got this.

Time for sweet sleep (Proverbs 3:24).

Living With Expectation

I hope you cherish your own fingerprints of God. I plan to watch for more. I don't understand all of life, but I trust the Lord with my eternity, so I can trust Him with this short time on earth.

Looking back, I see the fingerprints of God in every miraculous birth of my three sons; every baptism, every birthday party, football game, basketball game, wrestling meet, scraped knee, and broken bone.

What a tremendous honor to be a mother.

God Was There

It comforts me to know God was with Austin when he had cardiac arrest. He wasn't alone. We are never, ever alone. Sometimes I felt alone, especially at the beginning of the grief season when the pain was intense. When I didn't know what to do, I would bow down on the floor and just stay there, asking the Lord to help me, to fix me. He did.

It would be a year later when 1 Peter 5:6-7 jumped off the page into my heart. "If you bow low in God's awesome presence, he will eventually exalt you as you leave the timing in his hands. Pour out all your worries and stress upon him and leave them there for he always tenderly cares for you."

Later, I'll share a dream that changed my life. I know my son called out to the Lord, and in a nanosecond, he was absent from the body and present with the Lord. (See 2 Corinthians 5:8).

God didn't take my son from me. Rather, he took him to heaven. He rescued him. There are over three hundred titles for God in the Bible, and I want to know Him in each capacity. Right now, I've come to know Him as The Rescuer. He rescued Austin, and he's rescuing me from the pain of grief. He wants to rescue us all.

The Promise

In Luke 23:40–43, we see Jesus' crucifixion and His mercy. The thief on one side of Him **mocked**. The other **believed**:

"Jesus, remember me when You come into Your kingdom."

Jesus replied, "Today you will be with Me in paradise."

The best promise on earth. But let's not wait until our last breath; eternity is long.

Life is better **now**, walking hand in hand with the Helper.

Let's focus on the love God gave us through His only Son.

It outweighs the pain of goodbye.

No, wait! Let's just say, "See you later."

A Quarter and a Cart

One day as I was driving, I realized the terrible weight of grief was lifting. I thought, *Now, how can I focus on someone else's gain, not just my loss?* Knowing we reap what we sow, I wanted to sow hope.

A brief time later, leaving the grocery store, I left my grocery cart unchained so the next customer wouldn't have to put a quarter in the slot to unlock the cart. It was just a tiny way to pay it forward. Then I drove about sixty seconds across the street to the gas station. I parked, opened my car door, and there on the ground was a quarter. I smiled and picked it up. A very quick reaping! A fingerprint of God. I guess it's time for *change*.

One More Thought

If God names every star, and He does (Psalm 147:4), He can surely heal broken hearts. He can infuse hope where none seems possible.

And indeed, He can rebuild a life.

KEY TAKEAWAY:

God ordains circumstances and perfect timing to assure us He's present. He's helping. You are never alone.

MY JOURNAL

MY JOURNAL

MY JOURNAL

Chapter Four

A MARVELOUS GOD DREAM

Wrestling Champion

God-given dreams can bring divine encouragement. They shift our perspective forever.

Do-Overs

When my three sons were little, they often talked about do-overs. Whether they played checkers, shot baskets, or wrestled in the living room, I often heard, "I get a do-over!"

Have you ever wanted a do-over? I know I have. The good news is, I believe we can have one, or several if necessary. We can't go back in time, but we *can* go forward. We can start new chapters in life, fresh chapters. Following what feels like demolition we have an opportunity—yes, I said opportunity—to reframe our lives to fit what's happening now. Like it or not, grief ushers in a new normal... abnormal. So, picture yourself holding a beautiful crystal frame and place it gently around your *now*.

New Garments for a New Season

With a new chapter comes new garments, like putting on a new coat to step out in comfort and style. After all, we wouldn't run errands in a swimsuit when ten inches of snow cover the ground. We need to recognize our season so we don't get stuck. Seasons of life change, and change calls for action. The old garment slips off and heads to a thrift shop.

Remember the shredded wrestling shirt I mentioned earlier? Well, the Lord gave me a life-changing dream about that shirt, and I received a new garment. An exchange, the new for the old. That dream rocked my world in the best way.

Riding home with one of my sons after a whirlwind of closure events in Iowa, we recognized that our lives would never be the same having laid his brother to rest. I told him, "I *must* hear from God to find complete and total peace. I must!" Matthew Seven teaches us to ask and we will receive. So, I asked. A few days later, God answered with a dream that changed my life. It felt as real as this very moment, every color, every word, every smile, and *the gift* remain etched in my memory. I will never forget.

Journal Entry – The Dream

I dreamt about Austin last night. I stood behind a large brick gymnasium, much like one at the high school my three sons and I once knew. The building sat high on a hill, the football field stretching out below. My youngest son stood quietly to my left, my middle son to my right, as we all watched several doors close along the back of the building. Deep down, I knew Austin was inside. I ached to see him, to talk to him, as if we'd left something undone before his departure. Still, I hesitated. I didn't know if he was allowed outside, and I didn't want to cause him trouble.

Suddenly, one door swung open, revealing boys in sweat suits and wrestling singlets working out. My heart leapt, I was certain Austin was just beyond them. Desperate not to miss this chance, I called out quickly before the door closed, "Austin?" Instantly, a loud, familiar, "Yo!" answered back.

Moments later, Austin appeared. He stepped outside — healthy, radiant, college age, maybe, holding something in his hands, His smile lit up the space between us. With both hands, he handed me a small black box, just like the one the funeral home had given us, the one that held a beautiful candle with his picture on it. Months later, I realized the box said, "Life's Journey."

As I opened it, the box expanded, and out came a brand-new, gray, luxurious wrestling sweatshirt, soft like chenille. Across the front, in bold letters, it read, Champion Wrestler. Austin grinned and said, "This one's a lot better, Ma!" I gasped, "Oh, it's so beautiful!"

After giving me this wonderful gift, Austin stepped back, leaning casually against the brick wall, arms folded, serene, smiling as if to say, "Mission accomplished." A little further down, his coach had come outside, leaning against the same wall. One by one, more wrestlers emerged, lining up along the wall as if waiting to greet their families. Then, in a blink, Austin and his coach were gone. My sons and I stood there, hearts full, washed in a deep, steady peace. End of dream.

Wrestling with Life

When I woke, my heart soared. I had seen Austin, heard his voice, felt his presence. The dream stayed vivid and alive. I believe with every fiber of my being that Austin is with the greatest Coach of all time, in heaven.

Austin wrestled from kindergarten through college. I keep his shredded wrestling shirt from his university because it is a treasure to me. I'll pass it on to his children one day. I like it because it exemplifies the blood, sweat, and tears of his journey. Its glory days have ended, but the story it tells remains.

I find it fascinating that the gifted shirt in the dream didn't say *Wrestling Champion*. It said **Champion Wrestler**. There's a huge difference. Never give up.

Now, I'm the one who must keep wrestling, pushing through grief, finding my way to victory. I'm the one who needs to train, eat well, and get my strength back. The gift has made wrestling with life my responsibility in my new season. I know my role. It filled me with hope, and hope is not wishful thinking. The biblical translation is "the joyful anticipation of good." *Cling to hope* and be careful not to lose yourself in the chapter you're in now. This is not the end of your story.

Garments in Scripture

We see the significance of new garments throughout both the Old and New Testaments, our roadmaps for life.

In the Old Testament, the concept of new garments appears subtly, yet with meaning. New garments often marked status. For instance, Jacob gives his son a "coat of many colors" in Genesis Thirty-seven as a sign of his father's favor. Jacob sensed his son would step into a divine season as he envisioned amazing plans for him. Our Heavenly Father often wants to make upcoming changes visible to us and to others by giving us new garments.

Then there's Joshua who stands in filthy garments in Zechariah Chapter Three until God replaces them with brand new garments, splendid robes. This scripture reveals God's forgiveness and transformative power.

Moving Forward

In Matthew Nine, Jesus uses the metaphor of a new patch on an old garment to teach about incompatibility: "Who would mend worn-out clothing with new fabric? When the new cloth shrinks it will rip, making the hole worse than before."

This reminds me of grief. How can we move forward while clinging to the old? We can't. Hanging on to pain too long makes the hole in our heart worse. I'm not talking about forgetting precious memories, we cherish those. I'm talking about placing memories, both good and bad, in proper perspective so love fuels us forward instead of draining us from pain. Gratitude for what we had and still have can give us fresh perspective. The seasons have changed, ready or not, and we must change our garments with the seasons. Either we navigate life, or it navigates us.

Putting on the New

The Apostle Paul urges believers to put on a new life: "And he [Christ] has taught you to let go of the lifestyle of the ancient man, the old self-life, which was corrupted by sinful and deceitful desires that spring from delusions. Now it's time to be made new..." (Ephesians 4:22-23).

Again, Paul writes in Colossians 3:9-10: "Lay aside your old Adam-self with its masquerade and disguise. For you have acquired new creation life which is continually being renewed into the likeness of the One who created you, giving you the full revelation of God."

Taking off the old garment and putting on the new empowers us. It's a choice, a choice that transforms everything. We can all experience renewal through the power of the one true God.

Discernment and the Power of God Dreams

God communicates to us in many ways, dreams being one of them. So how do we know if a dream is from God or not? We learn. And it is crucial to write down or record our dreams immediately when we awake. If you think you'll remember and write the dream down later, you probably won't. Dreams evaporate. So, when they're from God, we honor them and write them down. The more faithfully we do this, the more dreams we receive, along with deeper revelation and understanding.

The Scriptures are full of examples where God gave people dreams. Even Joseph received a dream before Jesus, the Savior of the world, was born. There are some dreams I believe are an overspilling of our soul. When our mind and emotions are on overload, there's a restlessness that takes place, and rather than sleeping deeply, our subconscious seems to work overtime. Having dreamt for decades, I also know the difference between a God dream and a pizza dream. The dream I shared with you is the most vivid of my life. I can revisit it anytime, and nothing ever changes. I cannot alter it, even with a sanctified imagination, nor would I want to. I remember the colors, the sounds, the voices, every detail. It truly was an encounter that changed my life, and I remain forever grateful.

Jacob Wrestles with God

In Genesis Twenty-Three, we see Jacob resting by a river. When nighttime falls, he wrestles with a divine being. Some theologians believe the being was an angel; others interpret it as God Himself. The two struggle through the night, and by dawn, Jacob's life changes forever.

As morning approaches, Jacob's hip dislocates, but he refuses to give up. His tenacity leads to blessing, and he receives a new name:

Israel, meaning "one who struggles with God." The new name marks a transformation that *unfolds in the dark*. Jacob not only gains a new name but also steps into new destiny.

Jacob had lived as a deceiver, so God giving him a name meaning "one who struggles with God" carries deep significance. Sounds to me like his life was reframed. His family and all his possessions moved ahead of him, and there he stood, alone with God. Still, he held on. He kept wrestling and declared, "I'm not letting go until You bless me." Oh my, we sure can relate to that!

Wrestling, Redemption and Responsibility

We all wrestle with God at times. I know I did when I lost my firstborn. It's not that I didn't love the Lord, I did. It's all just so difficult, so painful. My whole world shook to the core. Let me encourage you to hang on, just like Jacob. He wrestled through the darkness until a beautiful sunrise broke through.

We all face wrestling matches and pivotal moments. Do-overs during that crucial time depend largely on choices. We can lie down and get stuck to mat, or we can rise up, wrestle, and win. I promise you; life exists beyond death. Redemption remains possible, and great faith can be restored. I've been thinking about what my new name should be. God and I will probably be the only ones who know it, but it's important to me.

Jacob walks away from the encounter with a limp showing that life is fragile, but that's okay. The frailty reminds us to hug others longer, appreciate them more, and remain grateful for what we *do* have. We all carry stories and wrestling with life proves hard, but it humbles us and forces us to either grow or fade. Our limps also remind us of our divine encounters and how they've changed us.

They make us more empathetic, hopefully kinder, gentler, and more tuned into the pain around us so we can become instruments of healing.

A Transformed Legacy

Jacob's actions after the encounter reflect this newfound purpose and responsibility. His reconciliation with his brother, which follows soon after, reveals his transformed state. That act not only restores their relationship but also sets a precedent for future generations, emphasizing forgiveness and unity. Jacob's role as a patriarch solidifies, and his story becomes a foundational narrative for an entire nation.

We're not letting go until God blesses us! We hang on, we begin to dream again because without a vision, people perish (Proverbs 19:18). We make wise choices moving through the stages of grief.

And now if you'll excuse me, I need to go and order a very special sweatshirt.

KEY TAKEAWAY:

Try to keep moving. Reframing and renewal don't come by standing still. They come when we wrestle through grief. Ask God for guidance and receive the "new garment" He has prepared for you.

MY JOURNAL

MY JOURNAL

Chapter Five

STAGES OF GRIEF

Personal Reflection

Walking through stages of grief together through a lens of experience. These are not magic stages to healing, but rather a guide to show us where we're at in the process. A guide to help us know we're not crazy, we're grieving.

Dear Austin,

Today felt difficult. Some days are hard, and some are harder. Grief experts say acceptance comes in time. I'm trying to believe that.

Guess what? We have something new in common now. I'm trying to reach the acceptance stage of grief and learn to live just one day at a time praying the serenity prayer you kept in your office:

God grant me the serenity
to accept the things I cannot change;
courage to change the things I can;
and wisdom to know the difference.

If I think beyond twenty-four hours, I can't bear the permanence of never seeing you again here on earth. I must remember that

Christians don't die, we simply change our address. Someday, my address will change, and we'll have our eternal home together as your brothers and many others join us, one by one.

BTW—Are you enjoying seeing family and friends up there? Oh, I bet you are! You always loved visiting and sharing stories with people. What a miraculous testimony you must have to tell! I can only imagine you shouting: "God is faithful! He never gave up on me! He never leaves us; He never forsakes us."

This morning, I watched the tribute video the funeral home created for us, photos of you from childhood to raising your own children. There have only been a handful of times in my life when a little shockwave moved through my body. Today, when I opened your video, marked one of those times. I guess my emotions remain raw. Healing takes time, so I'm not too concerned. Grief is the price of love. I'll get through it somehow.

The stages of grief shift constantly, so for a while this morning, it felt like I slipped back into stage one—hock. "You're really gone. You're not coming back. I want to see you!"

I loved watching you grow up with your two brothers. I feel so honored to be your mom. I learned to appreciate and enjoy your somewhat dramatic personality; we all did. I remember when you were a little boy, if you were sick, we all knew it—smile. Just the opposite of your middle brother, he could be sick and never mention it. If you felt excited about something, we all knew that too and joined right in. That's one beautiful thing about life; we can embrace every personality. We love the good things that made you, you.

I love you,

Ma

Over and Over

One painful thing about grief is we don't just lose someone or something once, we lose them again and again. When my son is absent from events, when I want to call him, when I have exciting things to share and can't, over and over it hurts.

I can understand why people get angry at God. And more importantly, He understands. But the reality is He's our lifeline. Hang on. He's the one True God that created the entire universe and *promises* to heal the broken hearted (Psalm 147:3). Period. I cling to that promise and try not to waiver. That word has become my anchor when I feel unstable. I know it's a process, so I trust the process.

It's so important to self-reflect and be *honest* with ourselves about our feelings. We don't want to get lost in any stage of grief. I've seen that. It's not pretty, and often a victim mentally settles in. Being stuck prevents emotional and spiritual growth and people allow themselves to become victims. Victims get attention but they don't get healed. Psalm Twenty-three reminds us that we walk *through* the valley—not get stuck in the valley. When we can acknowledge bad feelings, then good feelings can also be acknowledged, appreciated, and enjoyed as we move forward with life.

Grief Stages and Experiences

In 1969 Elisabeth Kübler-Ross wrote *On Death and Dying*. In her book, she introduced stages of grief. Since then, people have rewritten those stages umpteen times. I'm sharing my personal reflections of grief here, hoping they help someone find their way. It's a journey, not a race.

One thing that surprised me was how much the stages of grief vacillate. We may think we've completely finished a particular stage, only to find ourselves back in it. That's okay. Grief brings an emotional roller coaster. Over time, it does level out. Here are the stages I experienced.

Shock

I believe shock acts as a survival instinct, a gift from God perhaps. It may not feel protective, but it is. Your mind gives your heart time to catch up with truth. In the early days of grief, the intensity of pain felt almost, *I repeat*, almost unbearable.

When grief first hits, shock moves in. We feel numb and struggle to believe what just happened. I actually thank God for this stage. It sheltered me when I needed shelter. For a season, the dulling of pain helped me endure reality. This stage often lasts several weeks as we adjust to new surroundings.

I learned to stay cautious during shock. Some days, I couldn't immediately recall my phone number or my bank password. One of my sons once said he drove into a cul-de-sac and asked himself, "Now, how do I get out of here?" Shock is real.

Denial and Pain

For me, denial slipped in immediately. Remember when the Sherrif's office called to tell me my son was gone? I kept saying, "No, no, no." Every part of me refused to believe my son was deceased. As the days passed, denial remained. My brain refused to accept the death of my son, so I didn't even try to push through the denial right away. I just let it be. That gave me a chance to grieve one step at a time, one day at a time, only facing as much as I could handle.

Eventually I needed to face denial head on since denial stands for not even knowing you're lying. I acknowledged it, and it began to fade. Reality settled in, pain did too. Oh my, so much deep pain. The suffering felt intense, and even though I knew suppressing it would be unhealthy, I don't think I could have squashed it if I tried. Diving into work or anything else to avoid the pain felt almost impossible. Pain took over for a season. I could manage a trip to the grocery store, maybe church for an hour or a family lunch, but that was it. And as soon as I walked back through the door at home, the tears came. I had held myself together as long as I could, and the flood returned the moment I sat alone with the Lord.

Everything in my life felt shaky and scary. I knew isolating myself wouldn't help, and yet I felt so cut off from the world, disconnected. How could everyone around me keep going as if life were normal when it clearly wasn't? It felt like being in a telephone booth screaming but no one could hear me.

In trying to identify what I felt during denial and pain; I landed on tremendous sadness and fear. This sadness went deeper than anything I had ever known. Through the years, I had learned to take the word *why* out of my Christian vocabulary because I understand we can't always explain the ways of God. But during the pain and confusion, *why* returned. I don't apologize for that; it was a part of the journey. It was honest. *Why my son? Why? Take my house, my car, all of my possessions, take me! Please, please don't take my son. What had I done to deserve this?* I worked hard all of my adult life. I faithfully served God and people, learning to love even the unlovable, and now I stood shattered.

Of course, when we ask questions through the filter of pain, what we really want is for the pain to stop. We're not always looking for answers, we're looking for relief. And the truth is, we don't always get to make perfect, logical sense of everything that happens. Sometimes things don't add up. That's life.

Fortunately, as I moved further along in my healing of grief, I came to understand something hugely important: God didn't *take* Austin from me. He *took* him to heaven, to paradise.

I can live through pain knowing Austin will not have to. He'll never have to face the hurt or struggle of this world. There really *is* a much better place. And he's already there.

Bargaining

The bargaining stage of grief didn't last long for me, but it definitely showed up. It became a way to try to control the uncontrollable. "Lord, maybe that wasn't Austin's body in the cabin. Maybe it was an overnight guest, a friend who needed a place to crash." But the tattoo on my son's arm shut down my irrational bargaining very quickly. In this stage, I didn't want a do-over; I wanted to totally undo what had happened.

I realized early on that bargaining simply distracted me from the pain, and because I knew ruminating would only harm me, I refused to entertain it. We can't heal by constantly returning to what broke us. For example, if I woke up and found myself cycling through the negative thoughts, about something or someone, I got up. Boom. I refused to lie there and let negativity take over. Where the mind goes the body follows.

During this stage, I joined a grief support group. I needed community and reinforcement from others. I needed a safe space to process and try to understand shock, denial, bargaining, and anger. I felt helpless and feared losing more of my loved ones. Thankfully, my group included good listeners, people who didn't judge but accepted me exactly where I stood in the grieving process. Finding support has become crucial to sharing, understanding, and healing.

Walking also helped me. It didn't feel as natural as it had for decades, but I tried to discipline myself to **just go**. Listening to music while walking soothed my mind, body, soul, and spirit. Nature therapy seemed to be just what I needed. When I took walks, I ate better, felt better, and slept better. The difference was huge.

Anger

As reality settled in more and more, anger followed. Not rage, just anger at life in general. Why is this fallen world so unfair? Why didn't God change the plan? Why does addiction remain so elusive through the centuries, with no one offering real solutions? No one.

I felt angry at the medical model, angry at colleagues, bosses, family, and friends who didn't help and sometimes hindered. Couldn't they see my son was desperate for help? Why do we expect people to help themselves when they no longer can? I was even angry at myself. Surely, I could have done more to fix things. Surely, a mother should be able to protect her children, even adult children. I'm not saying my anger was rational, I'm saying it was a stage I needed to work through.

Once again, journaling, groups, and counseling helped me move through this stage. I've never been someone who gets angry often, and when I do, it doesn't last long. It rarely produces anything good, so I don't park there. I try not to let the sun go down on my anger (Ephesians 4:26).

Identifying our feelings and sitting with them plays a role in the healing process. How long do we sit with them? As long as it takes. Anger may feel painful, but sometimes it's necessary.

Depression

This stage caught me off guard. It crept in months and months after losing my son. I hadn't experienced depression in thirty years. I only shared my struggle with close family and friends, and it caught some of them off guard too. After all, I really should have "moved on" by now.

Early on, as I began to seek answers and understand what triggered the depression, I realized I was suffering from grief accumulation. I wasn't just grieving one loss, but several, stacked-on top of each other. I won't list them again, since I mentioned them earlier, but simply recognizing what was happening helped. The depth of those losses piled up, and my soul felt overwhelmed. I felt empty, and nothing seemed to help. For me, depression was moderate, but please be careful as you heal. Do not allow depression to take over. Seek help. Doing so is a sign of strength, not weakness. A sign of bravery.

In addition to leaning on my support network, something interesting that helped during this stage was a prompting to put a few photos away. Sounds so simple I know, but I realized I had been looking at them too much, too often. In fact, they started to interfere with my sleep, so I removed a couple of them from my bedroom. This change didn't diminish my love in any way; it simply gave my mind a chance to rest. A small step toward a big victory. Do I still keep photos around my home? Oh yes! Remember, I'm the one who stayed up all night looking at them.

Acceptance

As we move through the stages of grief, life keeps going. Over time, I found my footing again. I got back on a productive schedule and started managing daily life. But something in me wanted more. The empty chair wasn't going to change, so I had to. I knew I had to reframe my life, though I didn't know how.

My dear friend Sheri helped me through that part of the journey. She and her husband had lost their beautiful daughter just a few months after I lost my son. We often meet for coffee and chocolate. We talk through our feelings, laugh, cry, and encourage each other consistently as we rebuild from the wreckage. I thank God for her.

I don't think we ever truly "get over" losing someone we love. But we *can* make choices, real, intentional ones. We can choose to take one step forward, then another, and then another. And one day, we look up and realize, we've come a long distance. We're still in the race!

We no longer have to hold our breath through a luncheon just to keep from falling apart. The fog has lifted, and we learned to *cling to hope*. We grow stronger, emotionally, and spiritually.

I've come to see that the steady practice of making good choices can lead us to dream again, to feel inspired again. That sense of *what could be* starts to come back. And I for one want to live in a way that, if the loved ones I've lost could see me now, they'd be proud.

May our strength grow from our pain, and may our triumphs be shaped by what we've lived through. May our acceptance of reality for what it is, not what we wish it were, lead us to peace. Remember: We cannot go back. But we *can* go forward with Jesus and our loved ones in our hearts.

Stages of Grief

Shock
The initial response to loss, numbness, disbelief, and feeling overwhelmed.

Denial and Pain
Struggling to accept the reality of the situation, often accompanied by deep emotional pain.

Bargaining
Attempting to negotiate or find meaning, hoping to reverse or lessen the loss.

Anger
Feelings of frustration, helplessness, or resentment surface strongly.

Depression
Profound sadness, withdrawal, and reflection on the magnitude of the loss.

Acceptance
Gradual adjustment and finding peace with the new reality.

KEY TAKEAWAY:

The statistics are in. You have currently survived 100% of the trials in your life. Congratulations!

MY JOURNAL

MY JOURNAL

Chapter Six

THE SILENT HARVEST

I'm forever grateful that judgment isn't ours to make. Our true calling, our deepest honor, is to love unconditionally.

GUEST WRITER: *Francis Frangipane*

A Dream that Led to a Dream

About four weeks before my son passed, I had a dream so vivid, it felt more like a visitation than a dream.

In the dream, as I watched from above, I saw Francis Frangipane and myself talking on the phone. Years ago, I served in his ministry. We were smiling, our conversation seemed pleasant and unhurried. As we were about to say goodbye, Francis said, "Paulette, I love you."

His words took me by surprise, not because they felt wrong in any way, but because during my time in that ministry, out team worked in a culture of Agape love. The team was blessed to work in an environment where Christian love was present, and we chose our words carefully, guarding our testimony as men and women working side by side in a world that is always watching. Love was often expressed through service, prayer, and kindness, rather than personal declarations that could easily be misunderstood by the public

The dream ended, and I awoke suddenly. Before I could even gather my thoughts, the atmosphere in the room shifted. As I sat there, the Presence of God was overwhelming. It felt like butterflies in my stomach, multiplied beyond anything our humanness can understand. The intensity actually startled me, not with fear, but with awe. It was the kind of Presence that makes you want to fall to your knees, humbling whispering, "You are God … and I am not."

A Dream, A Presence, A Whisper from Heaven

The following days, I prayed about the dream, asking the Lord for understanding. I came to realize the dream wasn't about Francis at all, it was about our Heavenly Father's love. Francis had been a great mentor to me in years past, a spiritual father. I had the honor of helping launch his In Christ's Image Training that still goes around the world today. His teachings and books profoundly shaped my life. They still do. He and his wife, Denise, are beautiful, humble followers of Christ, the real deal.

Oftentimes God uses familiar faces in our dreams to carry a message we'll recognize and receive. The words "I love you" felt like a gift from heaven. I wondered why I needed this powerful reassurance at this time. It was reassuring, but it bothered me. I had no idea my life was about to change … forever.

Looking back now, I see the dream as a true gift. It was a whisper; God's Presence was the embrace. And both were His way of saying, *"You are not alone. I am with you."*

Nine days after my son passed away, I was taking a walk and all of a sudden, I remembered a dream Francis Frangipane had shared with the world years ago. It is profound, and I realized my dream led me to his dream.

Printed with permission:

THE SILENT HARVEST

Francis Frangipane

A few years ago, I had a dream in which I found myself inside the mind of a dying man. The man had been in a coma for some time; his family had been praying, but they did not know whether or not he had accepted Christ. All they were sure of is that, throughout his life, he had resisted their efforts to lead him to Christ.

In the dream, I became so acutely aware of the man's state of mind, that his thoughts, feelings, and struggles almost seemed my own. Although his eyes were nearly closed and his vision clouded, he could see his loved ones at his bedside. I watched as he tried to reach toward his family, but outwardly his arm never lifted. Perceiving his thoughts, I heard him speak their names, but no sound whispered through his lips. A loved one holding his hand asked, "If you hear me, squeeze." He heard and pressed his fingers against hers, but no movement was seen; his hand clearly remained limp. He was conscious, he could hear their prayers, he felt the warmth of their kisses on his face but was perfectly incapable of responding.

Death approached, and he knew he was unprepared for eternity.

The pride and isolation that had throughout his life stood guard over his heart were gone. A physical catastrophe had overtaken him. Death approached, and he knew he was unprepared for eternity. Submerged beneath his placid exterior, a war had raged for his soul, which the Lord won. Subdued by

71

the relentlessness of God's love, he was finally at peace. It was during his time in the hospital that he had silently prayed and accepted Christ as his Savior. I was watching his last effort to tell them as life ebbed out of his body.

Suddenly, monitoring alarms ripped through the muffled silence of the room. His heart beat one last time, and I found myself looking down at the body of a man who had just died. The room was buzzing with nurses, while his family huddled in a corner, grieving. The idea of their loved one dying without receiving Christ was more devastating than the reality of death itself. I stirred and then woke. Yet, just as I left the dream, the Lord spoke to my heart,

"Tell them he's with Me."

God is Good.

Although some time has passed since I first had this dream, I am increasingly aware that many of God's people carry a deep abiding heartache concerning the death of an unsaved loved one. Obviously, this dream does not apply to all, but there are some for whom this experience is divinely directed. Thus, I submit this to you in a general sense because the Holy Spirit has assured me, He will bear witness to your heart.

I have also felt an urgency to pass this dream to you. I am convinced that the Lord has an important work for you. However, the enemy has used this unresolved loss to sow doubt into your soul. Not only are you troubled about your deceased loved one, but you have doubts about God's love, as well as the power of prayer. As a result, your confidence in God has diminished. Yet, it is precisely at this time that you need to stand without doubt for other members of your family.

Beloved, though there are many questions about the mysteries of life, we must not let the unknown obscure the face of the known. God is good. We know God loves us because He sent His Son to die for our sins. Indeed, Jesus said, "He who has seen Me has seen the Father" (John 14:9). When we look at Christ, we see God, and we know that God cares, and He is good.

Additionally, some of us have lost loved ones in sudden tragedies, where they seemingly had no time to repent or turn to God. Let me remind you of those who have faced near-death experiences and tell of seeing their "life flash before [their] eyes." They say that the progressive movement of time almost stopped. I believe that, even in what seemed like a "sudden" death, time itself slowed to a crawl. There apparently was enough time in this altered state to see and ponder one's life—and to make a decision or even call upon the name of the Lord.

In spite of what we do not know about the mysteries of life, one thing remains eternally true: God is our loving Father. He does not desire that any man perish, and He will fight to save us, even to the moment of our death. Let us, therefore, cast our burdens upon the Lord, for He genuinely cares for us. And let us again run with endurance the race set before us, for He has promised, "the people who were sitting in darkness saw a great light, and those who were sitting in the . . . shadow of death, upon them a light dawned" (Matt. 4:16).

Lord Jesus, thank You for dying for my sins. Lord, there are many issues I do not know, but I do know that You are good. Those things I do not understand, I give to You. I trust you with my life and I put in Your hands the care of those I love.
—FRANCIS FRANGIPANE

Important note from Paulette Reed:

Francis Frangipane's dream is phenomenal. I know it was from God. I believe it helps many, many people around the world. I am blessed to share the dream and to give honor where honor is due.

However, I never want to give the mistaken impression that every person *automatically* goes to heaven. That is absolutely not the message of the gospel. Each of us must come to a moment in time when we personally invite Christ into our hearts. Let's not wait until tragedy confronts eternity.

John 3:3 (NASB) makes it absolutely clear: "Jesus answered and said to him, 'Truly, truly, I say to you, unless one is born again, he cannot see the kingdom of God.'"

KEY TAKEWAY:

In spite of what we do not know about the mysteries of life, one thing remains eternally true: God is our loving Father.

MY JOURNAL

MY JOURNAL

Chapter Seven

FIGHT THE GOOD FIGHT

Never Give Up

Watching someone fight the good fight for decades brings both joy and pain. Their perseverance can inspire us to keep going and fight like they did.

Unconditional Love

Unconditional love doesn't look at the worst in people; it looks at the best. The Lord also looks at the best—the heart (I Samuel 16).

In relationships, it's important to discern the real person from the enemy. If a voice does not speak grace, love, kindness, and forgiveness, then it is not the voice of Jesus. This realization makes it easier to love unconditionally. It separates truth from lies. We love the person, not the lies. We love the person, not rudeness, shouting, disease, control, or anger. *We love the real person.*

The world often tells us not to give too much: keep strong boundaries, let people make their own choices, and leave them be. There is wisdom in that, and to a point it's true. But the way of Christ calls us further to go the extra mile, to pray without ceasing, and to give generously. For in the end, love never fails. If others fight the good fight trying to never give up, why would we give up on them?

One of the deepest elements of unconditional love is giving it freely, without expecting anything in return. Often, we do receive love back, but the absence of expectation is what makes it truly unconditional.

As I walked through grief and poured my heart into my journal, I realized there would be nothing in return, my son was gone. Strangely, that realization brought freedom. Freedom to simply love, without condition.

Imagine a world shaped by that kind of love. We would see compassion flowing more easily toward neighbors, strangers, even enemies. And through that compassion, hearts and lives are transformed.

I realize there might be times when we need to love from a distance if a person is abusive or insists on being alone. But most often we find ways to consistently show our love, the love of Christ, and hope it will eventually change minds and hearts. First Corinthians 13:4-7 says it best:

- Love is large and incredibly patient.
- Love is gentle and consistently kind to all.
- Love refuses to be jealous when blessing comes to someone else.
- Love does not brag about achievements or inflate its own importance.
- Love does not traffic in shame or disrespect, nor selfishly seek its own honor.
- Love is not easily irritated or quick to take offense.
- Love joyfully celebrates honesty and finds no delight in what is wrong.
- Love is a safe place of shelter, for it never stops believing the best for others.

- Love never takes failure as defeat, for it never gives up.

Understanding the Battle

Life's battles can teach us that one of the most important aspects of spiritual warfare is knowing the enemy. When we recognize what's really happening, we know which weapons to choose, who to ask for help, and where true sanctified strength comes from.

I so wish more people understood spiritual warfare. If you think you're at war with a spouse, boss, friend, or an addiction, you're not. Not really.

Ephesians 6:12 reminds us:

"Your hand-to-hand combat is not with human beings, but with the highest principalities and authorities operating in rebellion under the heavenly realms. For they are a powerful class of demon-gods and evil spirits that hold this dark world in bondage."

The scripture is teaching us, warning us not to fight against people. We must learn about fighting in another realm, through prayer, and surrendering to the Living God, partnering with him. Wrestlers don't wrestle by themselves.

A Journey Through Grief and Strength

Grief visited my oldest son early on. At age ten, I remember him grieving deeply at the loss of a grandparent. As a teenager, he lost a close friend to cancer. In his early twenties, he nearly lost his leg—and his life. He was hospitalized for weeks, fighting a horrible infection, a wound vac and morphine always by his side. In his mid-twenties, he mourned another friend killed in an airplane crash. And, in his early thirties, our beloved friend, Jeff, left this earth way too soon. Life seemed cruel, and despite his sense of humor, it seemed Austin had a deep sadness that never went away. It would be many years after the hospitalization when he fully realized he had been conditioned to "push the button" whenever pain knocked on the door.

Even so, He never gave up. His heart simply stopped beating. When we cleaned out his cabin, his desk overflowed with manuals, textbooks, and certificates. One of my sons said, "It's like Austin went to college three times." Fortunately, his story isn't over as he dwells in heaven eternally, for love never ends and now we carry the torch.

Choosing Positivity

Austin and I often talked about flipping negative thoughts upside down, choosing to think positively instead. That's exactly what we must do with unhealthy grief and painful memories. Grief remains with us, but we decide whether it controls us ... or not. There's a clear line between who we were before grief and who we become after. Learn to love the new you.

Painful and negative thoughts need attention to heal. We certainly don't want to ignore our thoughts and feelings and become a society that dissociates while constantly scrolling through our cell phones. We must deal with our attitudes and behaviors. If negativity is left unchecked, it takes root and grows ugly. I've seen people steeped in offense, anger, bitterness, and negativity. It harms them and everyone around them. It fosters isolation and low self-esteem, convincing people they're frequently judged when no judgment exists.

Isn't it amazing that loving people live in a loving world, and hostile people live in a hostile world, the same world? Let's choose to be positive and help others do the same if we can. The law of attraction will then bring you more and more positive outcomes.

Oh, and the white buffalo story. Well, here's a fun fact: Buffalo charge into storms rather than flee. By confronting the storm, they shorten their time in it. Instead of wasting strength retreating, they endure the fury head-on and reach calm skies more quickly. You can do the same!

Cherished Memories

As I walk the path of healing, I *choose* to hold on to the treasures of memories, good memories. The moments that remind me of how love shines even when we're hurting. Here are a few for inspiration:

- That day, Austin and I picked up a table and chairs for his cabin. Driving back, one chair took flight out of his truck. My grandchildren and I laughed as Austin told me to **calm down**, hopped out, and tossed the chair back in.

- His lifelong love for cats. Months before he passed, one of his kittens was struck by a car. When I visited his home later, I noticed a tiny grave in his yard marked with a handmade cross. It revealed his tender, gentle side.

- He dug a deep drainage trench down his *long* driveway with a pickaxe. It was grueling work. It kept him focused and there were no gym fees.

- During the years I traveled to preach, I vividly remember him telling me, *"Ma, strengthen in the homeland, first."* I never forgot that.

- He ran with determination. After his passing, a female police officer shared how she sometimes saw Austin running and would stop to give him a bottle of water. That's the spirit of a true wrestler, fighting the good fight, trying to get healthy, no matter the cost.

- He remained gainfully employed throughout his entire adult life, becoming a skilled tradesman even in the face of tremendous hardship. There was no gold retirement watch, but there was plenty of grit.

- My grandchildren and I were making smores one evening. Their daddy loved bonfires. We all chuckled when we realized he had purchased marshmallows as big as snowballs. We laughed so hard trying to eat them. Goo everywhere. Sticky faces, messy hands, and loads of fun.

I hope you can make a list, too.

It will be waiting for you on the tough days,

to help you smile through the tears.

It will be waiting for you on the good days,

to help you be grateful and cherish what you had.

Fighting Through Grief

We too must fight the good fight. Remember: We want to go all the way through the dark valley and walk into victory.

During the early stages of mourning, I asked the Lord how to keep going when I felt no motivation. He reminded me: we move forward by faith, guided by discipline. For example, we take walks because they benefit body, mind, soul, and spirit, even when we don't feel like walking. Motivation can be fleeting, but discipline builds results and those results awaken motivation. In other words, discipline takes me to the gym, motivation meets me at the door. Be brave. Show up.

Beauty for Ashes

Jesus offers a divine exchange: beauty for ashes, joy for heaviness. Ashes can come from grieving lives lost, broken relationships, shattered dreams, or self-inflicted wounds.

We need to be careful not to cling to ashes because sorrow feels familiar, even strangely comforting. But constantly revisiting the wound can slow healing. The enemy wants to replay the trauma and loss, but once we recognize his strategy, we refuse to ruminate. Starve it, and it dies. Time to look forward, not back.

Giving God our ashes allows Him to restore us and give us beauty for our future. Everyone has ashes, wounds from life. The question is: what will you do with them? If you surrender them, God can transform them into something beautiful. Perhaps that beauty is found in the coexistence of joy and pain, each one giving greater meaning to the other. Nehemiah 8 says, "The joy of the Lord is our strength." Wow! His joy, our strength. We really must be careful then because if we lose our joy, we lose our strength. You will know when it's time to take back your joy.

I don't know what you're grieving—a lost loved one, lost marriage, job, or relationships. But I do know you have more living to do. Our lives certainly take some shocking turns, but as we fight the good fight and stay in tune to God's timing, we know when we're ready to get up and show up. When I first started writing this book, I quickly realized that the pain of grief was still too raw. I needed to pause so I could write from a place of victory. I'm so glad I waited.

What's right in front of you? Your bucket list and dreams are still valid even if they're altered. Dreams can be fulfilled at any age, and sequencing isn't as important as moving forward. I didn't attend Bible College until I was about forty years old, and it's amazing how that worked out. I would consistently hear shouts across the campus lawns from *much* younger students yelling, "Hi mom!"

Start dreaming. Start living.

I have a quote displayed in my home that my sweet grandson loves to read aloud:

Charlie Brown says, "Someday we will all die, Snoopy."

Snoopy replies, "True, but on all the other days we will not."

Wrestling with Life

We know that all struggles end; the problem is they don't always end in the way we imagined. Lord, help us accept the things we cannot change.

I've fought the good fight and wrestled with God, and I carry a limp because of it, and that's okay. Someone once said, "*Never trust a Christian without a limp.*" A limp shows you've been through something real, that you've wrestled with life and still hold on.

I'm not letting go until God blesses me. I believe in His promise of exchanging ashes for beauty. Nothing will ever replace my son, but I know he would want the best for me and his family. I can see glimpses of new possibilities ahead. No matter how heavy grief is, we all have enough hope to hope.

Moving forward means more than just holding onto hope, it also means releasing the weight of regret. In the quiet moments, it's easy to replay the past, rehearsing the "woulda, coulda, shoulda" of every decision and every missed opportunity. Yet regret can keep us stuck in yesterday when God is calling us into tomorrow. Let's take a look at how to live free from the trap of regret and receive grace for what was and courage for what's ahead.

KEY TAKEWAY:

You are brave. You are cherished.
You are deeply loved.

MY JOURNAL

MY JOURNAL

MY JOURNAL

Chapter Eight

WOULDA, COULDA SHOULDA

Watch out for the trap of regret. Here's a megaphone shout to move forward.

GUEST WRITER: *Sam Barber, Head Wrestling Coach*

United States Air Force Academy

Regret and Reflection

We all have regrets and missed chances in life. Sorry, but they're unavoidable. We just don't live in a perfect world, have you noticed?

It's natural, even healthy, to look back and reflect. But if we linger too long in the past, reflection turns into paralysis.

I've met people whose emotions got stuck along their journey. At first, when they begin to talk, it sounds like they're sharing something that happened last week or last month. But as the details keep spilling out, every little moment, every word, you suddenly realize they're describing events from twenty or thirty years ago. They live in a loop of pain and disappointment. It's awkward, heartbreaking, and worst of all, they don't even realize it.

Let's not do that.

Moving Forward

We cannot change the past, but we can shape the future. Yesterday is set in stone, but tomorrow offers wide-open choices. As the song says: *"Let it go, let it go!"*

So once again, let's flip negatives into positives and lies into truths:

Woulda says: I would have done it if I had the chance.

We say: *That chance may be gone, but new opportunities are on the horizon.*

Coulda says: I could have done better if only I'd tried harder.

We say: *Life isn't over. I'm going to keep giving my best.*

Shoulda says: I should have done things much differently.

We say: *I've learned valuable lessons that will guide me moving forward.*

Words That Heal

When grief shatters our hearts, we need words of comfort, encouragement, and grace to carry us through. An email I received from my son's university wrestling coach remains one of the comforting messages I treasure. It holds pleasant memories and speaks compassion. It touched me so deeply that it inspired the title of this chapter.

Printed with permission:

Ma'am,

My deepest condolences for your loss. Austin was a special person to me, and I will miss my conversations with him, his infectious energy, and the encouragement he shared with me and so many others. I share your faith and know I will see him again. Like so many, I have found this week difficult, processing the would-haves, could-haves, and should-haves, and wondering if there was anything we could have done to have more time with Austin.

You raised a good man who positively impacted everyone privileged to know him, whether for twenty years or twenty minutes. The deep respect and admiration were mutual, and perhaps that is why we stayed connected through the years, even across thousands of miles.

I will truly miss my conversations with him.

Blessings and prayers to you, his family, and his friends.

With deepest sympathy,
Sam Barber
Head Wrestling Coach
United States Air Force Academy

Letting Go of Regret

As time marches on, we must look back less and press forward more. Transformation waits ahead, not behind. Of course, most of us wish we had done some things differently, but wishes don't heal broken hearts. Hope does.

During seasons of loss, self-condemnation only deepens the pain. Beating ourselves up never brings healing. Instead, we must choose self-care, gentleness, and grace. When we stop revisiting *Woulda, Coulda, Shoulda,* we stop prolonging our suffering.

As a mother, I did my best. I chose to love unconditionally. My regrets taught me to hope for a future where I share more compassion, empathy, sympathy, and kindness. I've learned the beauty of helping instead of fixing, listening instead of judging.

We can't go back; sometimes there are no do-overs in life … or death. But we can lay down the burden of regret. When the time comes to move on, you will know, and allow *Woulda, Coulda, Shoulda* to lose their grip. We press forward with open hearts, courage, and hope.

Finding Purpose in Pain

Of course, we'd all like to avoid suffering if we could. We value our safety zones and creature comforts. But pain is unavoidable, so the only healthy response is to face it with courage.

The good news? When we process grief and trauma with support, we often emerge stronger than before. It's like running a marathon, building spiritual and emotional muscles as we go. Early on, it may seem impossible to believe, but healing proves it true.

When I walked through the valley of darkness, I felt like I lost myself. Later, I realized I had to meet the "new me." That new me found purpose in the pain, and so can you. If I were a betting woman (which I'm not), I'd bet a million dollars that you too can find meaning in your suffering.

The Power of Support

Build your support network, whether large or small; go for it. Healing alone is almost impossible. Join a local group, share your struggles with counselors, friends, or family. Read, write, walk, and pray as you climb out of the valley of darkness.

When we make it all the way through, we can walk alongside others facing similar struggles. We carry more empathy, grace, and love. We can learn to appreciate life more, deepen our perspective, and ask: *What's truly valuable? How do I really want to spend the rest of my time on earth? Do I know where I'll spend eternity?*

When life forges us in fire, we develop tenacity. Let's not let the "what if's" blind us to "what is." Right here, right now, what's in your hand that can begin to mold and shape your future, your new normal?

Choosing Hope

Your grief does not define you, and healing is a journey. Be patient with yourself and others. Remember: Seeking help shows strength, not weakness. I will never apologize for my deep feelings of grief. Even as a seasoned Christian I knew I had a broken heart that only God could heal. Even Jesus wept. (John 11:35).

Peace exists, and if you haven't found it yet, you're on the way. As we lay down regrets and move forward with hope, we discover the power of words. They can chain us to the past or launch us into the future. They can wound or heal, tear down or build up, speak death… or speak life.

In the next chapter, we'll explore how the words we choose shape not only our own hearts but also the lives of those around us.

KEY TAKEAWAY:

*Don't let Woulda, Coulda, Shoulda define your past,
let them inspire your future.*

MY JOURNAL

MY JOURNAL

MY JOURNAL

Chapter Nine

I WILL FEAR NO EVIL

❧❧

The Valley of Darkness

The Twenty-Third Psalm can be an anchor for all of us as we heal together. It's a set of promises to cling to while resting in God's presence and love.

Dear Austin,

Today I was thinking about your Psalm 23 tattoo. You had it for many years, and it was always a blessing to me. I remember how, even as a child, you loved that Psalm, and how upset you were when I said it was often read at funerals. That is still true, but it also gives us peace and life. It clearly ministered to your heart and gave you comfort.

Okay, okay you were right. It really is solid truth. The longer I live, the more I see how relevant it is in every season of life.

You had your own relationship with the Lord, as we all should, and I thank God for that. I know you struggled with "organized religion," as you called it, and I understand. God didn't invent religion, man did. Religion can become a set of laws and rituals that keep people from experiencing a real, personal *relationship with Christ, one of trust and intimacy with the One who made them in His image. You had so many questions about God, and He likes that. He has all the answers, and He wants us to seek Him just as He seeks us. I am eternally grateful that Jesus died on the cross to rescue you, Austin, to rescue all of us. He is The Rescuer.*

I wish I had asked you more about what Psalm 23 meant to you. I wish many things. May we never take our loved ones for granted. May we ask questions, listen deeply, record videos, and respect each other's opinions, especially when they're different from our own.

I wonder which words in that Psalm spoke to you most. That He would care for you, so you'd lack nothing? That He would lead you beside still waters when you were anxious? I'm glad you knew you didn't have to fear evil, for God was with you. I'm glad He comforted you, and that His goodness and love followed you all the days of your life. And now, my son, you truly do dwell in the house of the Lord forever.

Love you,

Ma

Finding Peace

We all walk through chaotic seasons, times of fear and uncertainty. May the truth of the Twenty-Third Psalm anchor us and keep us grounded, no matter what comes our way.

When I was in the deepest parts of grief, it was hard to focus or even read. So, here's Psalm 23 broken into small, bite-sized portions of nourishment. The Living Word is food for both spirit and soul, and it works supernaturally within us as we open our hearts to it.

Verse by Verse —Psalm 23:1-6 (NIV)

¹The LORD is my shepherd, I lack nothing.

God cares for his people as only he can, leading them through life with wisdom and love. Sheep are not easy to guide as they wander, often unaware of the dangers around them. But the shepherd knows those dangers and keeps watch, both gently and firmly, bringing his flock back to safety.

Because we have a loving Shepherd who cares for us, we truly lack nothing. He provides for our needs, and often there is more than enough to share.

Throughout the Bible, we see provision again and again. I think "I shall not want," as some translations render it, points toward simple living, the kind that brings contentment. There's no need to keep up with the neighbors, no pull to rush to the mall for the latest and greatest, no constant urge to upgrade or impress. Lacking nothing is, in many ways, a matter of perspective. It isn't about getting everything we want; it's about trusting we have everything we need. From that trust contentment grows.

Reflecting on provision, I think of "Austin's Cabin." Perhaps by most standards, it wasn't great, but to him, it was home, a place to land safely every night. After divorce, he made it into a warm, comfortable home and secured everything he needed for him and his children. He manicured the huge lawn, planted flowers, tilled a garden, and chopped tons of wood for bonfires. He cherished the simple life surrounded by acres of trees and wildlife. These are good memories I hold close.

The cabin became important to me because it was the last place I spent time with my son here on earth before he was escorted to heaven. Luke 16:22 tells us that for those whose eternal home is secure, angels will join us (escort us) on our journey to paradise.

✓ **Journal prompt. Write about what you have, not what you don't.**

2,3aHe makes me lie down in green pastures,
 he leads me beside quiet waters,
 he refreshes my soul.

These verses paint peaceful images we can carry with us, places we can revisit in our minds anytime, anywhere. As we walk through dark valleys during life, we remember there is an *inner peace* we can tap into. We draw from the peace of God, and our hearts and minds learn to rest, to release anxiety. This peace is not found in a prescription bottle; it is a supernatural calm that invites us to lie down in green pastures.

In seasons of loss and high stress, rest may not come easily. Yet Psalm 23 reminds us that rest is fundamental for healing and restoration. Rest comes with trust since sheep only rest when they feel safe, satisfied, and free from fear. We can trust the Good Shepherd. We can picture ourselves beside still waters and breathe deeply, releasing our burdens to Him who carries them for us.

Trusting allows us to step away from the chaos and picture ourselves beside beautiful, quiet waters, set apart from turmoil. We refuse to be permanently drawn into the eye of the storm, the swirl of pain and confusion. Instead, we find refuge in *His* peace.

✓ **Journal prompt. What's keeping me from God's rest?**

3bHe guides me along the right paths
 for his name's sake.

This is wonderful news. When a shepherd guides his sheep, he doesn't take them down an accidental path. He guides them on the "right" paths. This requires *surrender* on our part... to follow. His name's sake means that our direction will reflect His honor and His faithfulness. The road might seem rocky, scary, and unfamiliar. But it's none of those things to Him. He guides us! He's trustworthy.

✓ **Journal prompt. Can detours lead us to destiny?**

⁴ᵃEven though I walk
through the darkest valley,
I will fear no evil,
for you are with me;

Life definitely is not always green pastures and still waters. But the shadow of death is not the end of the story. We walk *through* the valley into a season of restoration and resurrection power.

When we're in a dark valley season, it's crucial to keep our eyes on the Shepherd and follow Him, not giving any power to evil. No self-medication, no self-harm or neglect, but self-care as we navigate the walk. We put our trust in the One who leads us to safety. It would be different if we were walking through the dark valley alone, but we are not!

We all go through dark valleys in life, times so challenging we're not sure how to make it through. But avoiding our feelings while in the valley is not helpful. Remember we talked about *acknowledging* our feelings because denial stands for not even knowing you're lying. Yes, oftentimes facing our true feelings takes courage but that's exactly how we get through the valley.

✓ **Journal prompt. How can I implement healthier types of self-care?**

[4b] *your rod and your staff,*
they comfort me.

The rod protects us, and the staff guides us. A shepherd uses these for course correction of wayward sheep. These corrections are not punishment, they are love. Knowing and believing this should bring us comfort. We can trust God and maintain peace knowing if we mess up, He will bring us back. Grace, grace.

> ✓ **Journal prompt. Have I ever mistaken correction for rejection?**

[5] *You prepare a table before me*
in the presence of my enemies.
You anoint my head with oil;
my cup overflows.

And yet another verse about provision. During difficult days it may be tough finding green pastures and still waters, but when it seems like adversaries are surrounding us, blessings are still available in the middle of the adversity, not only after it ends. And there they are, right in front of us so we won't miss them. A prepared table, a table of honor.

And when our cup overflows, we have the joy of giving to others. This helps us get our eyes off ourselves and onto others in need. Always a win-win with the Good Shepherd.

> ✓ **Journal prompt. How can I bless someone today even though I feel empty?**

[6] *Surely your goodness and love will follow me*
all the days of my life,
and I will dwell in the house of the LORD
forever.

It's comforting to know our Shepherd goes ahead to guide us on the right paths and even more comforting to know His goodness and mercy follow us all the days of our life. We are, in the best way possible, boxed in by His love. We're enveloped, surrounded on every side. His presence goes before us to guide and follows behind to protect. We can never wander too far where His love does not reach. No valley is so dark that His goodness and mercy do not encircle us.

What a wonderful promise to dwell in the house of the Lord. This is a promise of *now* and forever. Our shepherd's surrounding love and presence is our home in this life and our destination in the next.

✓ **Journal prompt. How can I live today with my eternal home in view?**

Dear Austin,

Today I was thinking about the ache of missing you. So many of us carry the weight of grief, but you do not. I once read a book about a man who was dead for several minutes and visited heaven. He said one of the most common questions he receives now is, "Do our loved ones in heaven miss us?" His answer was, "No, they're expecting you." Amazing. In eternity there is no time, so your expectation sustains my hope.

In some tiny way, I now understand a little of what Mary must have felt when her Son, Jesus, died. I cannot fathom watching Him be crucified, a cruel, agonizing death on a cross. This for a man who was perfect and without sin, fully God and fully man. In the Garden of Gethsemane, He prayed and sweat drops of blood, knowing the suffering ahead: the torture, the weight of the world's sin, an agony our finite minds cannot grasp. Yet He chose the cross, so that we could be set free. The nails did not hold him there, love did.

A part of me feels as though it died with you. But you are free, forever, and I will accept that exchange. That's the love of a mother, just as God proved the love of the Father when He gave His only Son, so that whoever believes in Him will not perish but have eternal life.

Love you always,

Ma

Resurrection Power in Dark Places

When the heavens and the earth were created (Genesis 1) the earth was formless, empty, and *dark*. Think about that. All of creation and humankind were created out of darkness.

About a year and a half after my son passed, I drove hundreds of miles to visit the empty cabin. I sat down where he took his last breath on earth and was escorted to heaven. I wanted to prove to myself and to the devil that this is not a place of death. Death died on the cross; Jesus gave us eternal life. The cabin is a place of resurrection power, a step that led to paradise.

May a creative miracle be born in the valley of darkness as you cling to hope and fight the good fight.

KEY TAKEAWAY:

We are free to walk, not run, through the valley of darkness and find our way for we fear no evil.

MY JOURNAL

MY JOURNAL

Chapter Ten

THE POWER OF WORDS

Life or Death

Words can seriously heal or harm.

Words Are Forces

For as long as I can remember, I've tried to live by and teach what Scripture reveals about the power of words. Words aren't just sounds; they are forces. They move across time and societies, shaping relationships, businesses, churches, schools, and nations. A single word can stir up courage or fear. Words can help heal a broken heart or deepen pain.

Words in Grief and Loss

I saw this play out after my son passed away. At the funeral home during visitation, my family and I heard many beautiful, comforting words; words that lifted us up in our time of grief. But not every word spoken that day brought life. One person even asked me, "Do you think your son went to heaven?" It's almost unthinkable, I know. Who would ask that of a mother crushed with grief? In another moment, a gentleman who was not a gentleman at all, made an inappropriate sexual remark. Again, hard as it is to believe, those words were spoken at such a tender time and caused more pain.

Choosing What to Hold On To

When grief and trauma crash into your life, you don't always process things clearly. You may find yourself stunned, thinking, *What just happened here?* For me, I chose to set aside those painful words quickly. I focused instead on the kindness and love being poured out by so many people around us. Days later, in prayer, I gave the hurt to God. I forgave, released, and blessed those who spoke foolishly. In truth, this wasn't my issue to carry, at all. Sometimes people just don't know better, and sadly, sometimes people want their words to sting.

Biblical Truth: Life and Death in the Tongue

Proverbs 18:21 (NASB) tells us clearly: "Death and life are in the power of the tongue." We must remember that what we speak has consequences. Scripture has always taught this truth, and like thousands of other biblical truths, the secular world, including psychology and communication studies, echo it. Words are powerful; they can impact mental health, behavior, and well-being.

The Psychology of Words

Think about it: affirming words can raise self-esteem and inspire hope. Negative words, on the other hand, can wound deeply, sometimes for life. A child who repeatedly hears "You're worthless" or "You're stupid" may carry those lies into adulthood, struggling to grow emotionally and in freedom and joy, bound by lies.

It's amazing that even a single word like *love* or *peace* can shift the brain, bringing calming thoughts and strengthening emotional stability. But hostile or careless words can trigger anger or fear, increase stress, and even impair decision-making.

Words in Relationships

And in our closest relationships, perhaps words matter most. Communication experts tell us that marriages, families, and friendships are either built or broken by the way we speak to one another. Encouragement, gratitude, and gentle words build trust. Careless remarks and constant criticism tear it down. Couples who regularly exchange kind words thrive more than those who speak negatively.

Warnings from Scripture

Again, the Bible has been telling us this all along. "Death and life are in the power of the tongue…" (Proverbs 18:21 NASB). This is not exaggeration; it's a spiritual reality. Words can breathe life by bringing hope and encouragement. Or they can bring death by sowing destruction, lies, and despair.

James 3:5 warns us about the same thing: "And so the tongue is a small part of the body, yet it carries great power! Just think of how a small flame can set a huge forest ablaze." A careless word can unleash consequences far beyond what the speaker intended. Jesus Himself said that God will hold us accountable for *every* word we speak (Matthew 12:36). Wow!

God's Creative Word

In the beginning, the Words of the One True God created everything as seen in John 1:1. "In the beginning the Living Expression was already there. And the Living Expression was with God, yet fully God." God spoke creation into existence: "And then God announced, "Let there be light and light burst forth" (Genesis 1:3)! Words are not mere sounds. They are power, divine power to create, to sustain, to redeem. Think about that sustaining power ... there is still light to this very day.

Speaking to the Grieving

Speaking the right words is so important when meeting with the grieving. In moments of loss, words can become tender tools. Silence can feel like absence and careless words can deepen wounds. Many who lost loved ones recall hearing a phrase like, "God must have needed another angel." Though well-meaning, such words can feel cruel during the pain of great loss.

Romans 12:15 tells us: "Celebrate with those who celebrate, and weep with those who grieve." That means standing alongside the brokenhearted, validating their pain, and offering words that comfort. Sometimes it's as simple as saying, "I'm so sorry for your loss," or "I'm here for you." A grieving heart may not be ready for theological explanations, but it can rest in the assurance that God is near: "The Lord is close to all whose hearts are crushed by pain" (Psalm 34:18).

The Damage of Careless Words

Words of gossip, slander, or criticism can inflict real damage. Proverbs 12:18 warns: "Reckless words are like the thrusts of a sword, cutting remarks meant to stab and to hurt. But the words of the *wise* soothe and heal." So it seems words can leave scars just like a real blade. And James 1:26 even says, "If someone believes they have a relationship with God but fails to guard his words then his heart is drifting away and his religion is shallow and empty." These are serious warnings!

The Beauty of Wise Words

On a positive note, Scripture also gives us a vision of what wise words look like: "Winsome words spoken at just the right time are as appealing as apples gilded in gold surrounded with silver" (Proverbs 25:11). **The right word, spoken at the right time, is priceless.**

Life-Giving Words

Here are three examples of powerful words to stir your soul:

- To a friend overwhelmed by failure: "Setbacks do not define you."
- To a colleague drowning in self-doubt: "You bring strengths to our team."
- To a grieving parent: "I can't imagine your pain, but I am here for you."

So simple yet so profound. Communication experts might see this as empathic listening followed with wisdom. The Bible simply calls it grace and truth. Either way, the heart should be the same: CCS – Care, Compassion, Sensitivity.

Stewardship of Our Words

Please: Let's remember that words are never neutral. They hold power to heal or hurt, to unite or divide, to bless or curse. Every word we speak either reflects Christ or denies Him. We are called to steward our speech. May our words carry grace, faith, and hope.

Moving Forward

Did I receive all the right words needed in my time of need? No, and you won't either. That's just not realistic. I wish life wasn't so hard at times, but it is—for everyone.

The good news is, when we're ready we move forward, and we can choose to learn to give what we once longed for and never received:

The right empathy, not just feeling another's pain, but standing beside them in it.

The right words, spoken with kindness and gentleness, when silence seems deafening.

The right sympathy when someone's world is falling apart, and they just need love.

Life has a way of teaching us through what we lacked. Every unkind moment, absence of comfort, missed word of encouragement become a reminder of what really matters.

Let's do better. Let's be the kind voice that calms; the person who listens and listens some more.

When we give what we did not receive, we can break old cycles. We can create new cycles filled with hope, compassion, and healing. In doing so, we find that *what we once needed has become what we give.* We can be a part, even a small part, of mending a heart.

KEY TAKEWAY:

I'm here for you.

MY JOURNAL

MY JOURNAL

Chapter Eleven

THE HEART

Mended and Trusting Again

The Master Potter reshapes what we think is beyond repair.

Rebuilding Emotional and Spiritual Trust

You've been there, really been there. You've got the scars, maybe even the T-shirt.

Heartbreak. Loss. Betrayal. The kind of pain that steals your breath and makes you wonder how the world can just keep spinning while your world has stopped. You sit there in the quiet, feeling raw and unsure of everything.

I want you to know, that's okay. You're not weak for feeling this way. You're human. You're healing.

When your heart takes a hit, something deep inside shifts. Your sense of safety, your belief in goodness, maybe even your faith, all of it feels shaky. And when the hurt comes from a place where you really thought God would step in … it hits even harder.

You might find yourself whispering, "God, where were You? Why did this happen?"

Those are sacred questions. They are words of grief and faith interwoven. You do not have to hide them. God is not offended by your honesty, and He isn't distant because you're struggling to understand. Never, ever forget, He draws near to the brokenhearted, even when words fail us.

"The Lord is close to all whose hearts are crushed by pain, and he is always ready to restore the repentant one" (Psalm 34:18).

Healing Is Messy

The road back to wholeness is never clean or predictable. It's not a straight line, and it definitely doesn't follow a schedule. Some days feel like you're moving forward, and others feel like you're right back where you started. But that's okay too, grace works quietly, from the inside out.

Healing often begins when you give yourself permission. Permission to feel what you feel, to cry, to question, to rest, to not be okay for a while. You don't have to rush your healing just to look strong or "faithful." God already knows your grief and your faith can co-exist in your heart.

Some days, faith seems like a whisper. Other days, it's just breathing in and out and getting through. Healing isn't pretending it didn't hurt, it's learning that pain does not get to define you or your future.

When Trust Feels Impossible

After deep hurt, even hearing the word "trust" can make your stomach twist a bit. Maybe you've built walls to keep yourself safe. You replay old conversations, preparing for the next letdown. Once, your heart was open and soft, now it feels like you've got armor on.

That's normal. It's self-protection. But those walls that keep pain out also keep love from getting in.

Rebuilding trust doesn't happen overnight. It's not blind faith; it's cautious courage. It's learning, little by little, that not every story ends in heartbreak. Not every person will leave. Not every season ends in loss.

And sometimes the first person you have to learn to trust again… is yourself.

To trust that your heart's wiser now.

To trust that God hasn't walked away.

To trust that love is still possible.

Taking That First Step

There's no magic formula for trusting again. You can think about it, pray about it, read about it, but eventually, you have to take that shaky, real-life step.

It might start small, like telling a trusted friend how you really feel, letting someone help you, choosing kindness even when you feel guarded, or whispering a small prayer when your heart's tired.

These might not seem like big moments, but they are. Every time you choose trust over fear, or hope over bitterness, you're rebuilding the foundation of your heart and your faith.

And please listen: If you wait until you feel "ready," you'll probably wait forever. The courage doesn't show up first, it shows up when you step out.

Vulnerability Isn't Weakness

We live in a world that boasts about "having it all together," but real connection, real healing, happens when we drop the act.

Vulnerability isn't saying "I'm weak." It's saying, "I'm brave enough to be real."

Pain may have changed you, but it didn't destroy you. Letting yourself be seen, tears, fears, cracks, and all is where love grows again. It's also where faith becomes personal.

Remember, even Jesus wept. Vulnerability can be sacred.

Grieving With Hope

There's a phrase I love—"*We grieve with hope.*"

It means we don't ignore the pain; we just refuse to let despair have the final say. We cry, but not as people without faith. We ache, but not as people without a future.

Hope doesn't erase grief; it redeems it.

It whispers, "There's still beauty ahead, even if you can't see it yet."

"To strengthen those crushed by despair who mourn in Zion to give them a beautiful bouquet in the place of ashes, the oil of bliss instead of tears, and the mantle of joyous praise instead of the spirit of heaviness" (Isaiah 61:3).

Sometimes hope is loud and bright. Sometimes it's just a quiet breath in the dark. But even on the days you can't seem to hold onto hope, *Hope Himself is holding onto you.*

Rebuilding Emotional Trust

Healing your heart is about slowly reteaching it that it's safe to *feel* again It's safe to turn off autopilot. It's okay to love, to be loved, to show up fully.

A few gentle reminders to help navigate a journey you didn't want to take:

✓ **Take your time.**

✓ Healing isn't a race. Don't let anyone rush you. Trust blooms slowly, like spring after a hard winter.

✓ **Start small.**

✓ It's the little things like showing up, telling the truth, setting boundaries, forgiving yourself. Every small choice matters.

✓ **Name your fears.**

✓ Saying out loud, "I'm scared to be hurt again," doesn't make you weak. It makes you aware. And awareness is where healing begins.

✓ **Let God into the messy parts.**

✓ You don't need fancy prayers. Just talk to Him: "I'm angry." "I'm confused." "I'm tired." He already knows; He wants to walk with you through it.

✓ **Let joy back in.**

✓ Joy isn't always laughter. Sometimes it's peace, gratitude, or just noticing goodness like a sunrise, a warm cup of coffee, or a text from a friend. Let those moments remind you: life still holds beauty.

Rebuilding Spiritual Trust

When your heart breaks, your faith can feel fragile too. You might still believe in God but struggle to trust His goodness. That's normal. Faith after pain looks different, quieter, more honest, less polished.

It's not about pretending everything makes sense. It's saying, "God, I don't understand all of this, but I still want to walk with You. And when I can't walk, thank You for carrying me."

That kind of faith grows in the waiting, in the tears no one sees, in the moments when you open your Bible even though you feel numb and it feels heavy.

Quiet faith isn't weak faith. Sometimes, the strongest faith doesn't shout, it just keeps showing up.

"Now may God, the inspiration and fountain of hope, fill you to overflowing with uncontainable joy and perfect peace as you trust in him. And may the power of the Holy Spirit continually surround your life with his super-abundance until you radiate with hope" (Romans 15:13).

Let Love Heal You

Love is not the opposite of pain; it's the answer to it. Grief is love.

Let yourself be loved, slowly, safely, fully. Let kindness in. Let compassion in. Let grace in. Each act of love, whether it's a hug, a prayer, or even your own self-forgiveness, helps mend your broken heart.

Transformation

There's something sacred about being broken and rebuilt. You're not who you were before the pain, and that's okay. Maybe the "after" version of you has softer strength, deeper empathy, and a clearer sense of what matters.

When God puts a heart back together, He doesn't just glue the pieces; He creates something new, something beautiful. You become like elaborate stained glass, and your light can shine through the cracks. Our healing reminds us of "kintsugi" ... the Japanese art of repairing broken pottery with lacquer dusted or mixed with powdered gold, silver, or platinum, highlighting the cracks rather than hiding them. Amazing!

Your scars don't disqualify you from love; they prove you've loved deeply.

Your tears don't show weakness; they show life.

And your story, the one that's still unfolding, might just help others find their way through the dark valley.

Trusting Again With Hope

So where do you go from here? Maybe you take one small step. You reach out again. You pray again. You open your heart just a little more.

You won't do it perfectly; none of us do. But every step toward trust, even the shaky ones, says, "I'm still alive. I still believe."

Here's the truth: God never wastes pain. He didn't waste the horrendous suffering of His Son who became the Savior of the world, and He won't waste yours. He restores. He rebuilds. He breathes new life into what felt gone for good.

You **will** laugh again.

You **will** love again.

You **will** trust again.

Not because everything suddenly makes sense, but because grace meets you right in the mess and leads you on to live in victory.

One day, you'll look back and realize that what broke you also taught you about peace that surpasses all human understanding (Philippians 4:7).

So keep going. Keep hoping. Keep trusting.

Because Love never gives up on you.

KEY TAKEWAY:

The only way to trust again is to trust again.

MY JOURNAL

MY JOURNAL

Chapter Twelve

LIVING IN VICTORY

Not the Agony of Defeat

Redefining victory. Not escaping suffering but learning to endure with grace and weave joy and pain together into our tapestry of life.

Signs Pointing to Victory

When I was in the throes of the deepest pain of my life, it was *intense.* I remember wondering how I would ever make it through such anguish. How could I possibly overcome this and move forward?

But then, subtle signs began to appear, little indicators that healing was happening, that God truly was at work mending my heart. One of the clearest signs was when I started to dream again.

I began to ask myself: *What could my future look like as I embraced my new normal? How might I turn this pain into purpose? How could I help others who are walking through their own valleys of darkness?*

Those questions were evidence that hope was stirring again.

I believe the same will happen for you! Don't overlook those small glimpses of light, those gentle nudges of life returning. Maybe it's the thought, *"I think I'll take some flowers to the neighbor who had that fall,"* or *"Today I'll send a get-well card to my boss."*

Those seemingly small acts are not insignificant. They're proof that you're healing, that you're becoming present again, that you're **living.**

What Really Is Victory?

When we hear the word victory, we often picture winning as the crowd cheers, the medals shine, and the story ending with triumph. The struggle is over, and we've come out on top.

But maybe victory is something deeper than that.

Maybe it's not just about winning in the way the world defines it, but about learning, growing, and trusting even when the outcome looks different than we hoped.

Maybe victory sometimes looks quiet, invisible to others, but real and alive in our heart.

So, let's walk through this idea together, openly, with hope. Let's see if we can find a kind of victory that brings comfort to the broken, courage to the weary, and peace to the ones who feel like they've lost too much.

Victory in Sports

Sports give us a clear picture of what the world calls winning. There's a scoreboard, a finish line, a celebration. Yet, if you talk to the athletes themselves, they'll often tell you that their greatest victories weren't the ones that earned medals.

Their real victories came in moments of endurance, showing up after injury, pushing through discouragement, refusing to quit when it would've been easier to walk away.

Think of the underdog team that didn't win the championship but found strength, unity, and joy in the journey. *Now, that's victory.*

Or what about the runner who comes in last but crosses the finish line after months of recovery and pain? The crowd might not notice, but heaven surely does.

Victory, in life and in sports, is often not about the outcome, but about the courage to keep going. And maybe that's the lesson we carry into everyday life. Each day we rise again after disappointment, each time we extend grace when we'd rather give up, those are small, sacred wins. Every unseen act of perseverance is a victory written in eternal ink, not in headlines or trophies but in the quiet places of the heart.

The truest champions are not always the ones the world applauds, but the ones who choose integrity when no one is watching.

Victory in Faith

In our Christian walk victory takes on an even deeper meaning.

It's not always about getting what we asked for or seeing prayers answered the way we hoped. Sometimes it's about trusting God in the silence, believing He's still working even when we can't see the whole plan.

The greatest victory in all of history didn't look like victory at all. When Jesus hung on the cross, it looked like failure. Yet three days later, the resurrection turned the darkest moment in the history of humankind into the brightest dawn in all of time.

May that remind us: sometimes victory is hidden in what feels like loss. Sometimes our tears water the seeds of miracles we can't yet see as ashes turn to beauty.

As Paul wrote, "We are more than conquerors through Him who loved us" (Romans 8:37). So even if we don't feel like conquerors every day, in Christ, that's who we are. Victory isn't a score we earn; it's an **identity** we're given.

This kind of victory brings freedom; freedom from needing everything to go our way to feel complete. It releases us from comparison, from constantly measuring our worth against others.

True victory in faith is quiet confidence in God's goodness, even in unanswered questions. Knowing that when seasons in life are bad, He is still good. It's saying, "I don't understand, but I trust You." It's about cherishing the memories that nothing can ever take from us, the love, the laughter, the random acts of kindness. It's finding peace in knowing that every battle we face has already been redeemed by the One who conquered death itself.

When Prayers Aren't Answered Our Way

It hurts when we pray, sometimes for decades, for healing, for reconciliation, for direction, and the answer doesn't come. Or it comes in a way that we really don't care for at all.

But that doesn't mean we've lost.

It doesn't mean God has forgotten us.

Even Jesus prayed, "Father, if you are willing, take this cup of agony away from me. But no matter what, your will must be mine" (Luke 22:42).

Surrender opened the door to the greatest victory the world has ever known.

So when your prayers aren't answered your way, you're invited into a different kind of victory, the victory of trust.

Trust that God's love holds you steady, even when life shakes.

Trust that His story is still unfolding.

Trust that nothing is wasted, not even your pain.

There's beauty in surrender because it shifts our focus from control to communion. Sometimes God's "no" is a redirection toward a greater "yes" we couldn't have imagined, and the waiting becomes holy ground when we realize that even in unanswered prayers, He's shaping our hearts into Christlikeness.

A Win-Win Reality

Here's the quiet beauty of life in Christ: no matter what happens, we live in a *win-win* reality.

If prayers are answered, we celebrate God's goodness. That's a win. If life is hard and prayers *seem* unanswered, we lean into His strength. That's also a win. We know the end of the story and God wins, so we win. We know where we will spend eternity, and that's a humongous win.

Even in death, we win, because death has already been defeated.

"Where, O death, is your victory? Where, O death, is your sting?" (1 Corinthians 15:55 NIV).

This truth reframes every fear. It means that even in the face of loss, disappointment, or suffering, we are standing on victorious ground. The cross and the empty tomb remind us that **every ending in this life can be the beginning of something new, something eternal**.

Overcomers

To overcome doesn't mean we never struggle. It means we keep walking, even with trembling hands. It means darkness doesn't get the last word.

Scripture reminds us:

"You see, every child of God overcomes the world, for our faith is the victorious power that triumphs over the world" (1 John 5:4).

"Never let evil defeat you, but defeat evil with good" (Romans 12:21).

To overcome is to keep faith alive, even when hope feels fragile.

A New Way to See Victory

Victory is saying, what an honor it is to be a mother, a son, a daughter, a friend.

Victory is running the race, even if you finish last in the world's eyes.

Victory is choosing to trust God when the answer is not what we want.

Victory is finding inner peace in the midst of chaos.

Victory is remembering that **the cross turned death into eternal life**.

Victory is hope that whispers, *"This is not the end. Hang on!"*

So if you feel defeated today, please know, your story isn't over. What feels like your weakness can become your strength.

Living It Out

- **Redefine Winning:** Don't measure success by outcomes. Measure it by love, courage, and faithfulness.
- **Shift from "Why Me?" to "What Now?"** Let your pain become a place of growth. Let it draw you closer to God's heart.

- **Anchor in Eternity:** This life is not the final scoreboard. The victory that matters most is eternal.
- **Celebrate Small Wins:** You got out of bed. Victory. Offer kindness when you're hurting. Victory. Choose to forgive. Victory.
- **Lean on Community:** We were never meant to overcome alone. Let others carry you when you can barely walk.

Clinging to Hope

Maybe you feel like you've been losing for a long time—to illness, heartbreak, exhaustion, or silence. If so, let me whisper this: *you are not defeated.*

Victory isn't about never falling. It's about getting up again, even slowly. It's about walking **through** the valleys and trusting that light still exists, even on the days you can't see it.

Sometimes, the very places you thought would destroy you become the soil where your deepest strength grows and your scars can tell a story or endurance, not defeat. Victory often comes quietly, disguised as survival, as resilience, as grace in the middle of heartbreak.

Closing Thought

What if victory isn't just about winning, rather it's about becoming who you were created to be?

It's about finding beauty in brokenness, hope in heartache, and peace that passes all human understanding in the waiting.

Lift your head, friend. You are not forgotten, and you are not finished.

The scars on Jesus's hands and feet are marks of ultimate victory. The scars of life can be beautiful too, molding us, shaping us.

Remember, in Matthew 21 we see that *after* the darkest hour on earth, Jesus became the Savior of the world. He won victory over death, taking on our sins and offering us eternal life.

If we live, we win. If we die, we win. Live well.

> ## KEY TAKEAWAY:
>
> *You are an overcomer, beautifully, quietly, eternally victorious.*

Dear Austin,

We'll meet you
at the gate.

Much love,
Ma

MY JOURNAL

MY JOURNAL

MY JOURNAL

Chapter Thirteen

THE CABIN

A Home that Led to a Gate

God has invited you to salvation and claimed you as his own. If you do these things, you will never stumble. As a result, **the kingdom's gates will open wide to you** *as God choreographs your triumphant entrance into the eternal kingdom of our Lord and savior, Jesus... (2 Peter 1:10-11).*

The Power of Choice

Every single day, we make choices, thousands upon thousands of them. Some studies say perhaps as many as 35,000 choices a day. Most of them we don't even notice like what to wear, how to respond to a comment, what to think about while we drive, what memories to revisit when the world gets quiet. But some choices are monumental, the ones that shape the direction of our hearts. Among the greatest of these is this: *what will I carry in my thoughts today?*

What an amazing gift God has given us, allowing us to choose which thoughts to nurture, which memories to hold close, and which ones to let go. Grief, especially, tests our choices. In the beginning, when the pain is raw, it seems like the grief chooses for us. The sorrow takes over our thoughts, our breathing, our rhythm. It feels as though it owns us. But over time, by the grace of God and through

137

His healing Spirit, we remember that we can *take thoughts captive*, just as the Word says in 2 Corinthians 10:4–5.

In that process, we realize something life-changing: we are not powerless. We can invite Light into dark places. We can exchange despair for hope. We can choose to remember **love instead of loss**.

If we dwell on horrible things, on the scenes that replay and wound us again and again, we're feeding thoughts that are **not** from the Lord. The devil delights in trying to keep us trapped there, believing there is no way out. But that's not what God wants for His children. He longs for us to seek His heart, His peace, to pray for His strength, to reach out for help when the burden feels too heavy.

He desires that we take steps toward *progress*, not perfection, not performance, but progress. Progress in healing. Progress in trusting Him again. Progress in growing into the best, most compassionate, most grace-filled version of ourselves that we can be. Progress that allows us to carry on the legacy of those we love, keeping their goodness alive in the choices we make each day.

A Mother's Heart

I am very aware that by many people's standards, Austin's cabin might not have seemed special. It was small, simple, tucked away in a quiet corner of the world. The wood was weathered, the roof a little uneven, and the furniture a mix of old and new. Someone driving by might not have thought it was special at all. But Austin called it home, and that made it special to me. Some people probably don't remember Austin as special either, not the way I do. But from a mother's heart, I see *all* of my family as great.

And that's **exactly** how our Heavenly Father sees *you*!

He doesn't measure greatness by the size of a house, a bank account, or a job. He doesn't look for flawless performance or worldly success. He looks at the heart (1 Samuel 16:7). The willing, imperfect heart that still beats with love and destiny. He loves you unconditionally!

Austin had a good heart. He cared deeply, worked hard, and laughed often. He adored his children. And even when life became messy or unbearably difficult, his heart stayed true. He *longed* to a good husband, a good father, brother, son, neighbor, and employee. Even as he wrestled with battles that sometimes kept those hopes from becoming reality, the desire was always there, steady, and sincere.

So yes, the cabin might not impress the world, but it's *great* to me. It's sacred ground, the last place on this side of Heaven where I spent time with my oldest son. We decorated together, hanging pictures and putting beds and bookcases together as he created a home. The kids painted the garage door, and we all worked on projects side by side. We argued a bit, and we laughed a lot. We bragged about the children, talked about dreams and ordinary things that now seem extraordinary.

And oh, the children, did I mention I have five perfect grandchildren in total? Each one is a miracle, a living reminder that life continues, love multiplies, and joy can be found again. When I see their faces, I see hope rising, even in the soil of sorrow. They carry the future.

From Darkness to Light

When I think of Austin's cabin, I don't see darkness. I see *Light*.

Because I know this truth as surely as I know my own name: because of God's saving grace, love, mercy the very moment, no, the very *nanosecond*, that Austin's heart stopped beating on earth, he was present with the Lord (2 Corinthians 5:8). The Bible assures us of that. I believe he was lovingly escorted into Heaven by angels, just as Jesus describes in Luke 16:22.

And now? Austin has no more pain. No more struggle. No more confusion, fear, or weariness. The weight he once carried has been lifted forever. He is whole, free, radiant. And I believe, with all my heart, that we, his loved ones, will join him one day, when the time is right. It's crucial to **know** where we will spend eternity. That's a long, long time.

We have hope to cling to. We have promises from the Lord that steady our feet when a wave of grief threatens to pull us under.

The Lessons of Grief

I think when we lose someone we love, we become students of grief learning to navigate intense pain. At first, all it seems to teach is how much something hurts. But slowly, gently, if we allow God to walk with us through it, grief starts teaching us how to see differently.

Grief teaches us gratitude for the moments we *did* have instead of despair for the ones we didn't.

It teaches us compassion for others who are hurting.

It teaches us patience—with ourselves, with the process, with others.

And perhaps most beautifully, it teaches us to *remember* in a new way.

We stop remembering just the ending, and we start remembering the middle; the A-frame home in the woods, the great hugs, the tiny miracles tucked into ordinary days. The smell of coffee in the cabin, the racoon looking in the patio door, the zip tie holding up a bunch of bananas, the beautiful Christmas tree on the deck and the children's stockings hung with care. We remember the laughter around the bonfire and the walks in the park with the kids. These are treasures no one can take away.

When the sadness comes (and it still does), *I try to meet it with love instead of pain.* I whisper a prayer. I remind myself that God is near to the brokenhearted (Psalm 34:18). I breathe in His peace and exhale my pain. Inhale, exhale. And then, I *choose* to think of something good. I choose love ... because that's what remembering can be—a sacred choice.

And eventually, time turns students into teachers.

The Path and the Gate

Sometimes I think of life like a long walk toward a gate. Along the path, there are homes, flowers, weeds, fields, dark valleys, storms, and beautiful skies. Each season leaves its mark on us. Some days we walk strong and sure; other days, we stumble and need to be carried. But always, always, God is with us.

When we reach the end of our earthly path, that's not the end at all. It's the beginning of our *forever.* The gate we reach isn't locked or cold; it swings wide, brilliant with light. Scripture says that God Himself choreographs our triumphant entrance into His kingdom (2 Peter 1:11). I love that word, *choreographs.* It reminds me of music, of grace, of beauty. Our homecoming isn't random or rushed; it's designed, purposeful, celebrated.

And when we step through that gate, we will see familiar faces waiting, smiling, waving, arms open wide. Austin Adam will be among them. Whole. Joyful. Free. I can almost hear his voice, *Hey Ma, over here!*

Choosing Hope Today

Until then, we live in the "already but not yet." Already held by God, already loved beyond measure, but not yet home. In this space between earth and eternity, we get to **choose** how we'll walk. Will we let bitterness rule, or will we choose gratitude? Will we focus on what was lost, or will we give thanks for what was given?

Each morning, when you wake up, you are standing at a tiny gate of your own, the gate of today. Each day the present is a present. Behind you is yesterday with all its pain and joy. Ahead of you is a new day, full of fresh mercy (Lamentations 3:22–23).

You get to choose how you'll walk through your *today gate*.

Choose peace.

Choose prayer.

Choose love.

Choose to think on what is good, right, lovely, and praiseworthy (Philippians 4:8).

When we choose to think positively, not in denial of our pain, but in defiance of despair, we heal. The light grows stronger. The memories soften into comfort instead of sorrow.

And one day, you may find yourself smiling at a memory that once made you cry. That's grace. That's the gentle work of God in a heart that refuses to stop **clinging to hope**.

The Cabin and the Gate

So when I think of *The Cabin*, I think of love. I have peace of knowing that, even in the darkest chapters of life, Light always wins. The cabin, to me, became a sacred place, **a place of resurrection life,** a home that led to a gate.

Through the ache of loss, I found an even deeper awareness of God's presence. Through the pain, I discovered new purpose. Through the tears, I learned to trust that joy would return and that there's a divine exchange available when we hand over our ashes for His beauty.

Maybe that's what *Austin's Cabin* really represents, not an ending, but a beginning. Not a goodbye, but a promise. A promise that the same God who met my son there will also guide us to our eternal home.

And when my time comes to walk through that final gate, I know I'll see Jesus face to face. I know I'll see many family members and friends and this time there will never be separation again. Everything will be brighter, brilliant, better, eternal.

Until that day, I'll keep choosing to remember the good times, to speak life instead of sorrow, and to trust the One who holds us all.

Because even now, in the quiet moments when the ache is still there, I can hear God whisper:

"You're not alone. Your story isn't over. The gate stands open and love never ends."

KEY TAKEAWAY:

When we reach the end of our earthly path, that's not the end at all. It's the beginning of our forever.

MY JOURNAL

MY JOURNAL

MY JOURNAL

Conclusion

THE FINAL FRONTIER

The Long Journey

I wish I could instantly take away your pain; I really do. Unfortunately, we know that's not the way life works. Each one of us must learn how to navigate journeys we never wanted to take.

Grief is not a quick visit; it's a long hike, and sometimes it seems to move ahead on its own terms. The good news is that healthy navigation is possible … even when it doesn't seem like it.

Each one of us must find our personal road to healing. Sometimes the increments of healing are tiny, sometimes they're big leaps of faith. Keep going!

Let's choose (there's that word again) to allow grief to make us **More**, not less. **Better**, not bitter. **Empathetic**, not cynical.

What Really Matters

Oftentimes, shock, grief, and loss can cause us to prioritize. That's a good thing. *What really matters? What is my purpose here on earth? Where will I spend eternity?*

I mentioned earlier that I have always disliked saying goodbye, but through grief I learned that not saying goodbye is more painful than saying it. For me, *see you later* works well, it fosters closure, and yet I know separation is temporary. It helps me move ahead and not get stuck in the dark valley.

Let's not be afraid to move forward as we grieve. It's okay. Where there was deep love there is deep grief, and that is the last act of love we have to give. Listen, moving forward can lead us to our loved ones.

What if each time we speak of our loved ones, they're whispering from heaven,

"Thanks for not letting my story end."

Your Story Isn't Over

The truth is, your story isn't over either.

Even in sorrow, your heart still beats with purpose. The fact that you're still here, still breathing, still seeking, means that God is not finished with you.

There are chapters yet unwritten, people yet to comfort, beauty yet to be discovered. Even if we can only take one shaky step at a time, each step matters. Each step counts.

Grief teaches us to live differently. It humbles us, softens us, rearranges the pieces of our souls. The things that once seemed urgent begin to fade, and the things that truly matter like faith, love, kindness, and connection come sharply into focus.

Grief clarifies what life seems to clutter.

Time Marches On

And as the days turn into weeks, and the weeks into seasons, we begin to realize something: **grief doesn't shrink, but our capacity to carry it grows.**

Grief does not shrink over time.

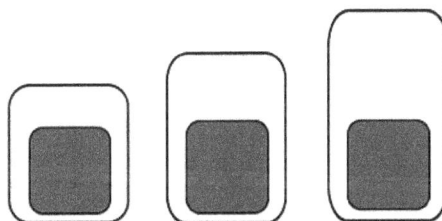

We grow around our grief.

We learn to hold both joy and sorrow in our heart.

We learn that tears and laughter can coexist.

We learn that grief is the price of love.

We learn that beauty can rise from ashes, and that love, real love, cannot die as we fight the good fight.

Quiet Strength

You may not feel strong right now, but strength often looks different than we expect. Strength is getting up when you want to stay in bed. It's making a meal, answering a phone call, watching another dawn breakthrough.

It's showing up for life even when you don't feel like it.

And over time, quietly, the fog continues to lift. The pain is still there, but it softens around the edges. Many memories that once felt sharp become warm again. You find yourself smiling at a song, or a scent, or a memory, realizing that the sadness has begun to weave itself into something sacred.

Beyond Loss

What lies beyond grief and loss?

A deeper perspective.

A wider peace.

A richer gratitude for every heartbeat we're given.

Eternity whispers to us in unexpected moments as a gorgeous sunset painted by the Creator, the stillness of prayer, the glimmer of a star that seems way too bright for coincidence.

And sometimes heaven sends the fingerprints of God to remind us that love continues, and we remember that death is not the end, it's merely a threshold.

Living Forward

Until we're all together again, we honor memories not by standing still, but by living fully.

By being kind even when it's difficult.

By believing in beauty again.

By allowing our scars to become testimonies and our heartbreaks to become sources of compassion.

Listen, the person you miss so dearly has already completed their race. They've crossed their finish line, and now they're cheering for you to keep going, "*Live, laugh, love!*" And guess what? If you don't do the first one, you can't do the other two.

So let's choose to be a CHAMPION WRESTLER.

Let's speak words that heal, not hurt.

Let's be present for the people who are still here.

And let's end each day with a thank you for another day of life.

A Glimpse of Eternity

Let's be one hundred percent positive that one day, when our own journey ends, we will take our final breath on earth and *our next one in heaven.* It's a choice, a powerful, eternal choice. Sin is deceptively subtle. It first appears as a friend offering some kind of comfort but later reveals itself as a thief seeking to steal, **kill** and destroy. If you stumble, Jesus stands as your advocate, declaring before the Father: *"I have already paid for that sin on the cross. I took the punishment so they could be free."* Believe that the price has been **paid in full** and let the Lord who conquered sin set you free.

Just think! Someday every tear will be wiped away. Every ache will dissolve into joy.

And in that sacred moment, you'll hear familiar voices and see familiar faces. You'll understand that Love really did win the battle between good and evil.

Until then, hold on to this truth: God wastes nothing.

Not one tear, not one prayer, not one sleepless night.

Every part of your journey is known, seen, and carried by a compassionate Savior who walks beside you **through** the valley and leads you toward the Light.

Grace Upon Grace

I pray you find comfort in small miracles, a soft breeze, a kind word, a song that arrives at the perfect time.

I pray you discover hope where you least expect it.

I pray you live in victory, not defined by humankind but by God.

I pray peace surprises you, wrapping around you when you thought it was gone.

You are not alone.

You are deeply loved, deeply seen, deeply understood.

And although grief may walk beside you, so does **grace**.

So, take heart. Take your time. Take gentle steps.

And remember this is not the end of the story.

Beyond grief is glory.

You're loved ones are expecting you.

The One True God who holds your loved one in heaven is holding you now, tenderly, faithfully, completely, guiding you toward that promised, radiant home where goodbyes are no more, and love is all that remains.

MY JOURNAL

MY JOURNAL

Addendum

CLINGING TO HOPE

"Even when your path takes me through the valley of deepest darkness, fear will never conquer me, for you already have! You remain close to me and lead me through it all the way. Your authority is my strength and my peace. The comfort of your love takes away my fear. I'll never be lonely, for you are near." —Psalm 23:4

"The Lord is close to all whose hearts are crushed by pain." —*Psalm 34:18*

"In the depths of my heart I truly know that you, Yahweh, have become my Shield; You take me and surround me with yourself. Your glory covers me continuously." —Psalm 3:3

"He heals the wounds of every shattered heart." —Psalm 147:3

"Don't worry or surrender to your fear. For you've believed in God, now trust and believe in me also." —John 14:1

"So now I'll lie down and sleep like a baby, then I'll awake in safety, for you surround me with your glory." —Psalm 3:5

"He understands humanity, for as a Man, our magnificent King-Priest was tempted in every way just as we are, and conquered sin. So now we draw near freely and boldly to where grace is enthroned, to receive mercy's kiss and discover the grace we urgently need to strengthen us in our time of weakness." —Hebrews 4:15–16

"Death is swallowed up in victory! He will wipe away every tear from every face and remove every trace of disgrace his people have suffered throughout the world, for the Lord Yahweh has promised it!" —Isaiah 25:8

"Lord, have mercy, for I'm in misery. My eyes are swollen with weeping; my body and are withering with grief." —Psalm 31:9

"He restores my soul." —Psalm 23:1

"Lord, you know all my desires and deepest longings. My tears are liquid words, and you can read them all." —Psalm 38:9

"What delight comes to you when you wait upon the Lord! For you will find what you long for." —Matthew 5:4

"Lord, listen to all my tender cries. Read my every tear like liquid words that plead for your help. I feel all alone at times, wandering like a pilgrim in this world." —Psalm 39:12

"My grace is always more than enough for you, and my power finds its full expression through your weakness…" —2 Corinthians 12:9

"Celebrate with those who celebrate, and weep with those who grieve." —Romans 12:15

"Those who sow their tears as seeds will reap a harvest with joyful shouts of glee." —Psalm 126:5

"Then young women will dance and be happy again, and young men and old alike will join in the celebration. I will turn their mourning into laughter and their sadness into joy. I will comfort them, making them radiant with joy instead of sorrow." —Jeremiah 31:13

"Lord, you are my lamp. You, Lord, illuminate my darkness." —2 Samuel 22:29

"I am convinced that any suffering we endure is less than nothing compared to the magnitude of glory that is about to be unveiled within us." —Romans 8:18

"Do not yield to fear, for I am always near. Never turn your gaze from me, for I am your faithful God. I will infuse you with my strength and help you in every situation. I will hold you firmly with my victorious right hand." —Isaiah 41:10

"So I say to my soul, 'Don't be discouraged. Don't be disturbed. For I know my God will break through for me.' Then I'll have plenty of reasons to praise him all over again. Yes, he is my saving grace!" —Psalm 42:11

"Pour out all your worries and stress upon him and leave them there, for he always tenderly cares for you." —1 Peter 5:7

"All praises belong to the God and Father of our Lord Jesus Christ. For he is the Father of tender mercy and the God of endless comfort. He always comes alongside us to comfort us in every suffering so that we can come alongside those who are in any painful trial." —2 Corinthians 1:3–4

"Are you weary, carrying a heavy burden? Then come to me. I will refresh your life, for I am your oasis." —Matthew 11:28

"Yahweh will always guide you where to go and what to do. He will fill you with refreshment even when you are in a dry, difficult place. He will continually restore strength to you, so you will flourish like a well-watered garden and like an ever-flowing, trustworthy spring of blessing." —Isaiah 58:11

"So he is able to save fully from now throughout eternity, everyone who comes to God through him, because he lives to pray continually for them." —Hebrews 7:25

"Live your life empowered by God's free-flowing grace, which is your true strength, found in the anointing of Jesus and your union with him!" —2 Timothy 2:1

"Cry out to me and I will answer you. I will reveal to you great things, guarded secrets that you never could have known." —Jeremiah 33:3

"Be strong and brave! Do not yield to fear nor be discouraged, for I am Yahweh your God, and I will be with you wherever you go!" —Joshua 1:9

"Do not be afraid of them, for I am with you and will rescue you, declares the Lord." —Jeremiah 1:8 NIV

"By his wounds we are healed." —Isaiah 53:5 (NIV)

"The Lord will fight for you; you need only to be still." — Exodus 14:14 (NIV)

"New, fresh mercies greet me with every sunrise. So wonderfully great is your faithfulness!" —Lamentations 3:23

"So, what does all this mean? If God has determined to stand with us, tell me, who then could ever stand against us?" — Romans 8:31

So Jesus went over it again, "I speak to you eternal truth: I am the Gate for the flock. All those who broke in before me are thieves who came to steal, but the sheep never listened to them. *I am the Gateway.* To enter through me is to experience life, freedom, and satisfaction. — John 10:7-9

And now, God, I'm left with one conclusion; my only hope is to hope in you alone! —Psalm 39:7

Endnote

1 WIKIPEDIA: Microchimerism is the presence of a small number of cells in an individual that have originated from another individual and are therefore genetically distinct. This phenomenon may be related to certain types of auto-immune diseases although the responsible mechanisms are unclear. The term comes from the prefix "micro" + "chimerism" based on the hybrid Chimera of Greek mythology. The concept was first discovered in the 1960s with the term gaining usage in the 1970s.

During pregnancy, a two-way traffic of immune cells may occur through the placenta. Exchanged cells can multiply and establish long-lasting cell lines that are immunologically active even decades after giving birth.

If this book supported you in any way, leaving an Amazon review may help it reach someone who needs it.

---

www.ingramcontent.com/pod-product-compliance
Lightning Source LLC
Chambersburg PA
CBHW052008090426
42741CB00008B/1599